Crisis Intervention
for Community
Behavioral Health
Service Providers
in Ohio

Books in This Series

Crisis Intervention for Community Behavioral Health Service Providers in Ohio

Overcoming Reluctance in Therapeutic Relationships

Psychotherapy for Families

Therapeutic Behavioral Services Using Interventions Based on Principles and Techniques of Cognitive Behavioral Therapy

Treating Attention Deficit Hyperactivity Disorder, Impulsivity, and Disruptive Behaviors in Children Using Behavioral Skill Building and Cognitive Behavioral Therapy Skills and Interventions

Treating Anxiety Using Cognitive Behavioral Therapy Skills and Interventions

Treating Depression Using Cognitive Behavioral Therapy Skills and Interventions

Treating Posttraumatic Stress Disorder Using Cognitive Behavioral Therapy Skills and Interventions

Crisis Intervention for Community Behavioral Health Service Providers in Ohio

TREATMENT MANUAL

Reinhild Boehme, LISW-S
Benjamin Kearney, PhD, *series editor*

THE INSTITUTE OF
FAMILY & COMMUNITY IMPACT

An OhioGuidestone Company
Berea, Ohio

Nothing contained in the manual is, or should be considered or used as, a substitute for medical advice, diagnosis, or treatment. The manual is not intended to replace, and does not replace, the specialized training and professional judgment of a health care or mental health care professional. Individuals should seek the advice of a physician or other health care provider with any questions regarding medications, personal health or medical conditions. This manual has been prepared as a tool to assist providers. In its efforts to provide information that is accurate and generally in accord with the standards of practice at the time of publication, the author has checked with sources believed to be reliable. However, in view of the possibility of human error or changes in behavioral, mental health, or medical sciences, neither the author, nor the editor and publisher, nor any other party who has been involved in the preparation or publication of this work warrants that the information contained herein is in every respect accurate or complete, and they are not responsible for any errors or omissions, or the results obtained from the use of such information. Further, the information presented in this manual does not constitute legal or financial advice or opinions. The ultimate responsibility for correct billing lies with the provider of the services. The reader should consult the current version of the relevant laws, regulations, and rulings.

The Institute of Family and Community Impact
An OhioGuidestone Company
www.OhioGuidestone.org

ISBN 978-1-7328190-2-3
Printed in the United States of America

Contents

Preface

For mental health professionals, building trusting relationships with clients and knowing which interventions will most benefit them are challenging enough. Helping clients who are also dealing at the same time with chronic conditions such as poverty, violence, and addiction can seem overwhelming. That's especially true for behavioral health service providers who have limited experience. That's why we at OhioGuidestone have developed this series of clinical manuals to help professionals develop their skills while providing effective treatment.

OhioGuidestone, the largest community behavioral health organization in Ohio, regularly trains new therapists and other behavioral health interventionists to work with clients who face severe, therapy-interfering challenges. We've brought that experience to these manuals.

In this era of managed care oversight, tight funding, and pressure to deliver evidence-based or informed care, it is essential for new therapists to get up to speed on best practices quickly. It is also essential for experienced clinicians to be well provided with effective and varied treatment plans. The manuals in this series provide step-by-step guidance on evidence-based and informed treatment modalities and interventions that can be used by both licensed and unlicensed mental health professionals—as well as by their supervisors for training purposes.

Seasoned mental health professionals will find the resources offered in these manuals useful for developing a renewed focus on evidence- and research-based interventions. At OhioGuidestone, our interventions are grounded in cognitive behavioral science and also shaped by the relational and attachment scientific advances that continue to inform the behavioral health field (especially the interpersonal neurobiology work published by W. W. Norton & Company). We understand the demands of serving client populations experiencing trauma and toxic stress. Our interventions are designed not to address discrete diagnoses (clients often have more than one) but rather the symptoms that are related to them. The series addresses a wide range of issues, such as depression, anxiety, ADHD, PTSD, and even reluctance to engage in therapy, and it provides interventions for children and adults.

We cannot "fix" our clients. But we can guide them along clear paths toward developing the skills they need to navigate the challenges they face, in their thoughts and in their lives. It's our sincere hope that the books in this series will help better prepare more mental health professionals to do just that.

— Benjamin Kearney, PhD, series editor

If you purchased this manual and want to make copies of interventions to help your clients, please do so. However, please do not share copies with other professionals but encourage them to buy manuals for themselves. This will help us continue to add to and update this series, to better equip all helpers who make a difference.

A Contextual View of Crisis

Crisis intervention constitutes an important part of treatment in the community mental health setting. Because many of our clients have been exposed to adverse childhood experiences (ACEs), they are more vulnerable to physical and mental illness. Additionally, our clients have been exposed to a greater than average number of ACEs: 55% of clients who completed the ACEs questionnaire between July 2016 and June 2017 reported having been exposed to four or more ACEs.

When providing care for clients in crisis in the community mental health setting, you should know that:

- Many of our clients have been exposed to developmental trauma, meaning that *trauma and toxic stress may have shaped who they are.* Many of our clients display a remarkable resilience despite their experiences. Resilience, however, can crumble over time and in the face of additional challenges, both internal (such as an emerging mental illness) and external (such as loss of housing or public benefits).
- They may have experienced poverty and the lack of supportive resources associated with poverty.
- They may suffer from co-occurring substance use disorders (SUDs).
- They may also come from marginalized populations that have been exposed to historical trauma.

Why does this matter?

In its Practice Guidelines (2009, p. 1), the Substance Abuse and Mental Health Services Administration (SAMHSA) aptly points out that crises happen not just because of mental illness, "but rather represent the combined impact of a host of additional factors, including lack of access to essential services and supports, poverty, unstable housing, coexisting substance use, other health problems, discrimination and victimization."

Crises happen in a context. In the case of community mental health, contexts merge to create conditions that can leave a client prone to crises.

If conditions of toxic stress and unprocessed past and current trauma are left unaddressed, our clients may become stuck in recurring episodes of crises that lead to further traumatization and even less ability to manage life's challenges. Our goal as service providers must not be simply to resolve the momentary crisis, but rather to "break the cycle of crises and advance the prospects of recovery for people with mental illness" (SAMHSA, 2009, p. 2).

This means that crisis intervention, at its core, is a complex service. It is not enough to avert a suicidal crisis (though that is already a tall order). We must also work to examine and alter the contexts in which this crisis developed. If external resources such as access to transportation are missing, then we must collaborate with the client and other providers to ensure that she can attend appointments.

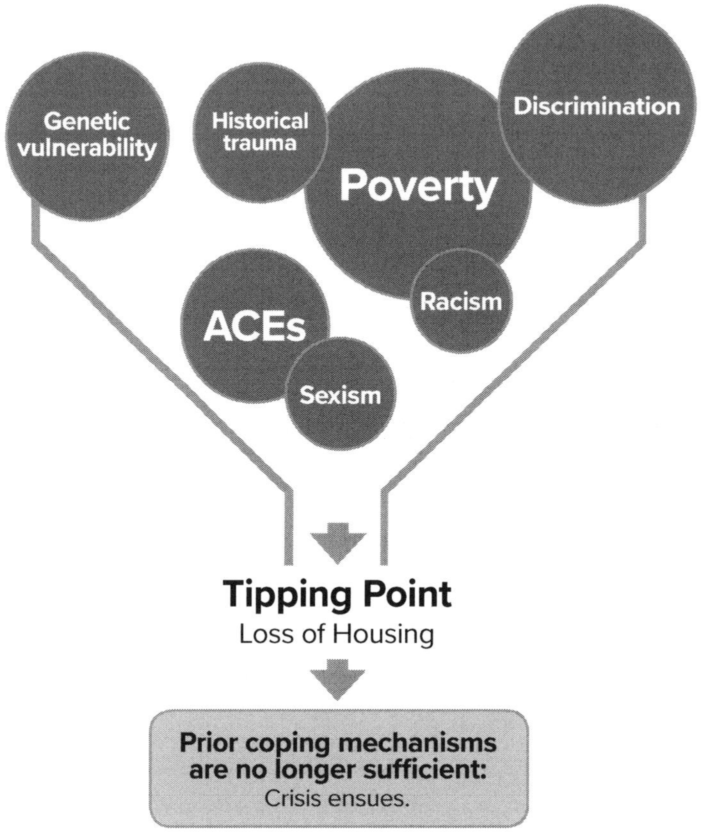

Figure 1

The following story illustrates how a confluence of factors can contribute to create a crisis:

> Renee is an outgoing 5-year-old who lives with her great-grandmother, Esther. Renee's mother is currently incarcerated for a nonviolent drug-related offense. Renee's grandmother is struggling with an opioid addiction and is not reliably present in Renee's life. When Renee was born she tested positive for several illegal drugs and was placed in her great-grandmother's care. Esther has cared well for Renee, and the child seems to be thriving. She cries frequently at night, and Esther does the best she can to console her. Renee also has nightmares and often crawls into Esther's bed. Esther struggles to make ends meet. She is retired and frankly too worn out from her life experiences to go back to work.
>
> When Renee begins to attend kindergarten, however, things begin to change. Renee struggles with learning and social relationships. She frequently steals from her peers and gets into physical altercations with them. Renee's

teacher is concerned about her ability to follow the curriculum and frequently keeps her in the classroom during recess to help her catch up. Renee is not grateful. After yet another unsuccessful attempt to write the alphabet, Renee kicks her teacher, swears at her, and runs out of the school. Because Renee has left school grounds, police are called. Renee stands on the edge of a busy street. She is crying and threatens to walk into traffic. Renee has reached her tipping point and so has her great-grandmother.

Remember that crises occur in a context. Renee's context consists of layers of toxic stress with islands of resilience and a very specific tipping point. Not every person experiences the same circumstances or responds in the same way. This is why truly understanding a client's contexts and circumstances, including exposure to trauma and toxic stress as well as resilience factors, is so important.

Does a contextual definition of crisis mean that people who do not live in poverty do not experiences crises?

Of course, anyone can experience a crisis. A person with substantial economic resources may be buffered for some time from reaching his tipping point. But perhaps his genetic vulnerability is high. Many factors and contexts can result in a crisis. Wealth and privilege can, but don't always, act as buffers.

It is important to gather information about context when providing crisis intervention. Here are some important questions to keep in mind:

- Does this person live under conditions of toxic stress and if so, what are those conditions?
- In what way is this person marginalized and how does this marginalization impact how she and her family respond to crisis intervention services and to you as a provider?
- How, specifically, did this person reach her tipping point? Identification of the tipping point can often lead to identification of urgently needed changes. In Renee's case, it is quite possible that she needs an assessment of academic and social and emotional skills that could lead to an appropriate school-based intervention plan such as an IEP (individualized education plan). With this plan in place and her needs met, Renee's symptoms are likely to diminish. It's truly amazing to see how people can blossom when their needs are met.

Crisis: A Working Definition

> A crisis ensues when a person's internal and external resources are no longer sufficient to manage a specific challenge and/or accumulating life challenges. When this happens, your client may become unable to cope and may become a risk to herself or others and thus require immediate intervention.

James and Gilliland (2017) define crisis as "the perception or experiencing of an event or situation as an intolerable difficulty that exceeds the person's current resources and coping mechanisms." When this happens, additional resources are needed to immediately assist the person in crisis. If these resources are not accessible, "the crisis has the potential to cause severe affective, behavioral, and cognitive malfunctioning up to the point of instigating injurious or lethal behavior to oneself or others" (p. 9).

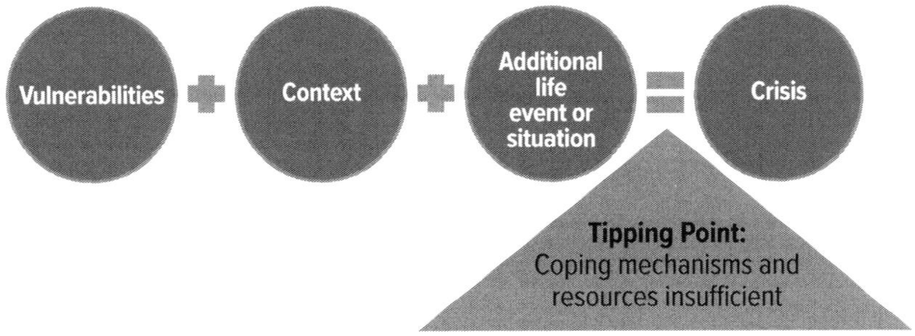

Figure 2

It is important to note that the term *perception* could be misinterpreted to indicate that the person experiencing the crisis is somehow misperceiving the situation as worse than it is, and that this indicates there is something wrong with her. It would be preposterous to demand that a client simply change "faulty" thinking when faced with compounding conditions of poverty, discrimination, mental illness, and resource scarcity. When providing crisis intervention, it is important not to discredit our clients' contexts and experiences. It is, however, our job to help our clients tap into resources and reconnect to inherent strengths, and thus build resilience. We need to validate our clients' experiences of marginalization and unacceptable conditions while, at the same time, also validating their lives as worth living and pointing them in the direction of hope.

Crisis Prevention

Crisis prevention must be built into client care, especially for clients with severe mental illness and/or a history of trauma and toxic stress.

In the best of all worlds, our clients would never experience crises because our services address their complex needs and wrap around them to build resources, resilience, and hope. When we are presented with a client who frequently calls after hours, experiences resource emergencies, struggles with emotion regulation, who is perhaps also abusing substances to "manage" his emotions, it is time to work on crisis prevention. Meet with your client. Identify all contexts and factors that contribute to the perhaps approaching crisis and create a workable plan to increase support, services, and resources. You may need to identify additional problems and make a note of those in the client record, and you should review the Individualized Treatment Plan (ITP) to add appropriate goals and methods.

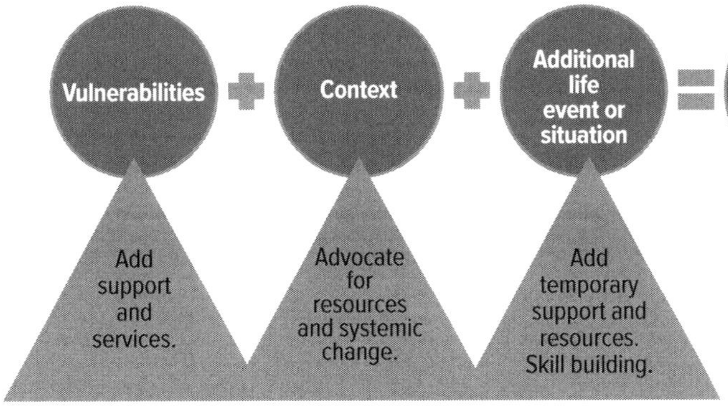

Figure 3

To create meaningful change within our clients' lives, we need to move from a reactive mode of services provision to planful prevention. This means that:

- We don't wait for a crisis to happen but plan ahead to prevent it.
- We create a meaningful and collaborative crisis prevention plan that is strengths-based and addresses service gaps.

- We recognize that systemic changes in service provision are needed and advocate for the removal of barriers to services.

Note that it is not always possible to avert a crisis, nor are you to blame when your client experiences one. But there is always something to be learned from a crisis. Here are some things to consider:

- Did I fully understand my client's various contexts?
- Did I openly address cultural differences and value them?
- Did I acknowledge and work to overcome, as much as possible, issues of marginalization and discrimination leading to service barriers?
- Did I engage my client cooperatively?
- Did I work to build upon inherent strengths to increase resilience?
- Did I manage my own emotional responses to this client effectively?
- Did I wrap all appropriate services around the client?
- Did I provide services in the client's preferred environment?
- Did I help my client expand her range of resources, both internal and external?
- Did I use supervision effectively to examine all of the above?

Crisis prevention is not a one-time event and goes beyond safety-plan creation. Crisis prevention examines how client contexts contribute to crisis development, identifies external and internal resource gaps, and works to bridge these gaps by wrapping all appropriate services around the client. Collaborate with your client to choose services. Services your client has chosen are much more likely to be successful.

Crisis Intervention Services

> Crisis intervention services address a life-threatening and/or complex emergent situation producing *extreme* emotional, mental, physical, or behavioral distress that *calls for immediate action.*

The State of Ohio uses a narrow definition of *mental health crisis*. It is within this definition that we can provide crisis intervention services. Clients who are enrolled in ACT (assertive community treatment) and IHBT (intensive home-based treatment) cannot receive separately billable crisis intervention services, as these types of services are built into both ACT and IHBT.

A crisis is defined as an experience related to a mental illness or SUD that:

1. Is a life-threatening situation.
2. Produces extreme emotional, mental, physical, or behavioral distress that *calls for immediate action.*

Immediate action is required when the lack of crisis intervention could result in serious harm to the client or other people. Here is an example of a situation that requires brief crisis-intervention services:

> Isaiah calls you and states that he is "in crisis." You ask screening questions about thoughts, plans, and intent to harm self or others. You also attempt to assess Isaiah's mental status. Isaiah does not give you much information other than stating, "I don't know what I am going to do. I might just end it." You determine that crisis intervention services are warranted. You quickly go to Isaiah's apartment and begin a formalized crisis assessment using the Columbia-Suicide Severity Rating Scale (C-SSRS, Appendix) and conduct a clinical interview. It becomes apparent that Isaiah has no plan or intent to harm himself. You contact Isaiah's therapist, therapeutic behavioral services (TBS) provider, and psychiatrist to ensure that appropriate follow-up will happen in a timely manner. Crisis intervention services now end. You have conducted an assessment of the crisis (which is permissible under Medicaid rules). As soon as you determine that the client is not at imminent risk for harm to self/others, the crisis intervention services end. In Isaiah's case it became clear within a short period of time, perhaps 20 minutes, that he was not at risk of serious harm to self/others.

To assess whether a client is experiencing a crisis, the mental health worker should determine

- whether the client has thoughts of suicide;
- whether the client has thoughts of wanting to harm others;
- whether there are safety issues in the client's environment;
- whether the client is experiencing overwhelming anxiety or panic and cannot control aggressive impulses toward self or others;
- whether the client is under the influence of drugs or alcohol;
- what happened to initiate the crisis and the individual's response to it; and
- the client's mental status.

For purposes of Medicaid reimbursement, the goals of crisis intervention are to ease the crisis, reestablish safety, and institute interventions to minimize psychological trauma (Ohio Administrative Code, 2018).

Activities may include but are not limited to:

- Emergent care
- Assessment
- Immediate stabilization
- Deescalation
- Counseling
- Care planning
- Resolution

It is important to understand that crisis intervention services, as defined in the Ohio Revised Code, are very short-term services. They address what James and Gilliland (2017, p. 9) refer to as the "behavioral emergency" that poses a threat to the safety of self and others.

Crisis intervention services are not meant to address a vague sense of lack of safety or feelings of anger toward another person. Crisis intervention services are called for when there is *a need for immediate intervention.*

The purpose of crisis intervention services is to:

- address the immediate root cause of the crisis;
- connect the individual to the most beneficial and appropriate services possible;
- return the client to his usual level of pre-crisis functioning; and
- facilitate access and continuity of care, including safety planning.

Crisis intervention services, as defined by the State of Ohio, take place at the tipping point, the moment when your client is running out of resources and coping skills and is beginning to pose a danger to herself or others.

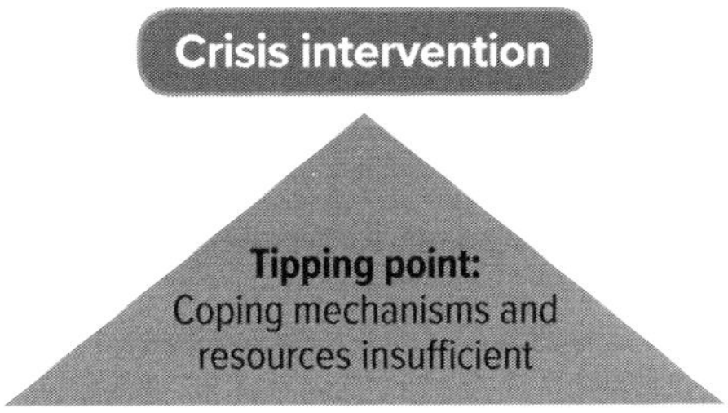

Figure 4

In other words: Your client may feel that she is "in crisis," but this does not always mean that crisis intervention services are warranted. Of course, other services should still be provided in an expedient manner.

You can find further information about crisis intervention services as defined by the Ohio Revised Code at www.codes.ohio.gov.

Here is an example:

> Jose is a 9-year-old who struggles with emotion regulation. His mother calls the crisis line and states that Jose "is having a crisis." She reports he is throwing his Legos at her and screaming loudly that he hates her. This has been going on for about 30 minutes.
>
> The crisis line counselor ascertains that no one is in immediate danger. Rather, everyone is agitated and at wits' end. The crisis line counselor determines that crisis intervention services are not warranted as no one is in immediate danger. She contacts Jose's community mental health worker, who agrees to a home visit before the end of the day. The community mental health worker also contacts Jose's mother immediately and helps her respond to Jose's challenging behaviors in a thoughtful manner.
>
> Later, when the community mental health worker meets with Jose and his mother, he is still somewhat agitated but no longer throwing things. The community mental health worker collaborates with Jose and his mother to create a plan for managing emotionally intense situations. Jose and his mother both feel like they are better prepared for the next time they have a disagreement and emotions flare up.

Where, then, is the line? At what point would crisis intervention services be warranted? Here are some indicators:

- Jose picks up a sharp object.
- Jose repeatedly screams about wanting to die.
- Jose moves toward the second-story window and threatens to jump out. (This, of course, requires an immediate call to 911.)
- Jose becomes incoherent and screams about ghosts telling him he needs to die (indicating that he is becoming psychotic).
- Jose's mother indicates that she can't manage Jose anymore and is about to "whop" him.

- Jose becomes catatonic and does not respond to anyone. He just stares into space.
- Jose walks out of the house and toward a major road without any regard for his surroundings, including traffic. This also requires emergency intervention: 911 must be called.
- There are any other indicators that the situation is becoming more dangerous and someone may get seriously hurt.

As you can see, not every difficult situation requires crisis intervention services as defined by the State of Ohio.

Lewis (2015, p. 588) puts it this way: "It is important for the clinician to remember that what separates a crisis from a difficult situation is the lack of tools and the perception of danger."

Because many of our clients have experienced conditions of toxic stress and trauma their "danger radar" may have reset to perceive danger in situations that may not actually pose an immediate threat to life and safety. This makes sense: If you have been hurt, or witnessed those close to you getting hurt, it makes sense to be prepared for danger at all times, because if you are wrong, you or your family could be hurt again. This is why it is so important to assess, as quickly and accurately as possible, if your client is truly in crisis or is experiencing difficulties. Difficulties with affect regulation, relationships, daily living skills, and the challenges of living under conditions of toxic stress require swift intervention and support—just not in the form of crisis intervention services as defined by the State of Ohio. The Danger Gauge (see following image) may be helpful in assessing if your client is in crisis or is experiencing difficulties:

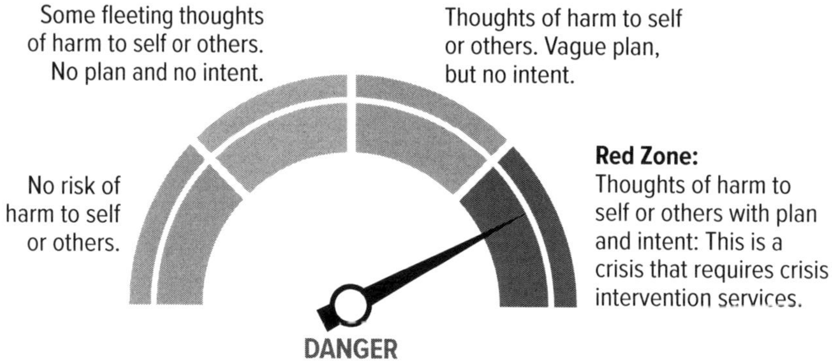

Figure 5

You can show your client the gauge and ask:

- ***How close are you to seriously getting hurt or hurting someone else?***
- ***Are you in the red zone?***
- ***If you are not, how close are you to the red zone?***

- ***Have you been in the red zone before? If so, when was this?***
- ***What is keeping you from moving out of the red zone?***

When your best clinical judgment tells you that your client is in crisis, you should provide crisis intervention services. If there is a need, and the situation allows, consult with your supervisor regarding the determination about the need for crisis intervention services.

For additional examples regarding the determination of whether crisis intervention services as defined by the Ohio Administrative Code are warranted, please refer to Appendix 1.

Crisis Intervention Services and Documentation

Remember: Timely and accurate documentation is required. Document concurrently using the electronic client record. If you are unable to document concurrently, complete your documentation as soon as possible. *All documentation must be completed within 24 hours of provision of services.*

In crisis intervention services, concurrent documentation becomes even more important. It can be difficult to remember everything that your client has said or done in a crisis situation. Crisis situations are stressful, and this can lead to you, the provider, forgetting about important details of the session. Here are a few examples:

- You are meeting with a client due to a suicidal crisis. Your client is extremely upset and you decide that you need to focus all of your attention on her. As a result, you don't complete your documentation concurrently. After the crisis concludes, you can't quite remember what the client said had triggered the suicidal crisis, because she said a lot of things quickly. This means that your documentation about antecedents for the crisis may be inaccurate. Even more importantly, if antecedents for the crisis are not accurately captured, documented, and addressed, it is unlikely that the safety plan accurately addresses client needs.
- You are meeting with a suicidal client. You are able to help your client deescalate thoughts of suicide, commit to safety, and agree to follow a safety plan. You talk about the important components of the safety plan, but it is getting late and you decide to come back the following day. You write in your case note that you verbally completed a safety plan with your client. The client, however, escalates into suicidal behavior and is hospitalized for a suicide attempt after your departure. Clearly, the plan you created verbally with your client was not effective. This is not surprising. During emotionally intense situations we may not remember as much as we normally do. Your client may have a vague memory of creating some sort of plan with you, but no recollection of the details. And now you have no documentation that proves that you actually completed a safety plan and that the client was in agreement.

Additionally, if you delay documentation until after your session concludes:

- You may be exhausted and delay documentation once more.
- Another situation may occur that requires your full attention, further delaying documentation of the first crisis and increasing the risk of forgetting what happened.
- Your client may experience an additional crisis. Documentation is now piling up and it may be difficult to recall the differences between the first and second crises.

Here is what works best:

- Use concurrent documentation. This improves accuracy and client understanding and involvement.
- Think twice before delaying documentation. If you find yourself delaying documentation often, work with your supervisor about integrating concurrent documentation into your practice.
- If you have delayed documentation, finish your documentation right after the crisis. Keep in mind that this is not permissible when it comes to safety planning, which is a collaborative process. Your client has to be with you and actively involved in creating a safety plan.
- If you have another appointment after the crisis, finish your documentation before the end of the day, or before you start seeing clients the next day.
- If you are struggling to complete your documentation within the required 24-hour time frame, call your supervisor. You supervisor will assist you with identifying a way to get documentation completed within the 24 hour time frame.

Principles of Crisis Intervention

Substance Abuse and Mental Health Services Administration (2009) has outlined principles for crisis intervention. The clarification given after each principle below is specific to crisis intervention services as defined by the State of Ohio.

1. **Access to supports and services is timely.**

   What this means: When a person is in crisis, meaning there is imminent risk of serious harm to self or others, services cannot wait. The crisis must be addressed right away.

2. **Services are provided in the least restrictive manner.**

   What this means: If possible, clients should be seen in their environment (this can, but does not have to, mean in their residence) to ensure that they are able to preserve connections to supports and culture. If possible, services should not be forced on clients. If clients can maintain safety with support at home, then they must be allowed to do so.

3. **Peer support is available.**

   What this means: During the acute crisis, if possible, the client should receive support from family and friends. When the acute crisis is over, the client should be connected with a peer support network such as a support group through the National Alliance on Mental Illness (NAMI).

4. **Adequate time is spent with the individual in crisis.**

   What this means: Crisis intervention must commence swiftly, but services cannot be rushed. We must take the time to convey genuine concern and conduct an accurate assessment.

5. **Plans are strength based.**

   What this means: While we must understand the skill and resource deficits as well as the stressors that led to the acute crisis, we must also build any intervention plan around the client's inherent strengths and abilities, which means we must help our client find strengths in the midst of the crisis.

6. **Emergency interventions consider the context of the individual's overall plan of services.**

What this means: Crisis intervention services must recognize contexts of toxic stress, marginalization, and discrimination, and be respectful of the client's cultural context and natural supports. Specifically, we must not put in place intervention plans that are not workable in or respectful of the client's context.

7. **Crisis services are provided by individuals with appropriate training and demonstrable competence to evaluate and effectively intervene with problems being presented.**

   What this means: You must have been trained to provide crisis intervention services. If you have been trained but are new to these services, you must have adequate support, including immediate telephone access to a supervisor.

8. **Individuals in a self-defined crisis are not turned away.**

   What this means: Those in a self-defined crisis may not fit criteria for the provision of crisis intervention services as defined by the State of Ohio. This means that crisis intervention services cannot be billed as such. We must, however, provide appropriate services to address the client's symptoms and problems. A client who is emotionally distraught but not a danger to herself may say that she is "in crisis." We can provide all appropriate services, just not billable crisis intervention services.

9. **Interveners have a comprehensive understanding of the crisis.**

   What this means: We must take the time to understand the crisis in its contexts. We must not reduce the client to a collection of symptoms and act on a superficial understanding of those symptoms.

10. **Helping the individual regain a sense of control is a priority.**

    What this means: By definition, an individual in crisis is experiencing a sense of loss of control. We must incorporate appropriate choice making into the provision of crisis intervention services. We should ask: Where do you want to meet? What would you like to see happen?

11. **Services are congruent with culture, gender, race, age, sexual orientation, health literacy, and communication needs of the individual being served.**

    What this means: We must strive to understand and respect the contexts of the client in crisis and approach this context from a perspective of humbly "not knowing." Instead of making assumptions about client contexts, we ask, humbly, about their contexts to strive to better understand them. This can be especially important in a crisis situation as lack of knowledge about a specific context can contribute to a misinterpretation of the nature of a situation or crisis.

12. **Rights are respected.**

    What this means: When a client is in crisis, it may be tempting to take over without explanation. Clients in crisis still have rights, such as the right to being treated in the least restrictive appropriate setting, the right to ask questions and receive answers, and the right to be treated with respect.

13. **Services are trauma informed.**

    What this means: Many of our clients have experienced and may still experience conditions of toxic stress related to marginalization, discrimination, and poverty, as well as trauma. We must ask: What happened to you? What got you to this point? What conditions contributed to this crisis? This assists with removing blame and shame and also signals that we are respectful of client contexts. Additionally, we understand that our clients may have a heightened response to stress and can interact in ways that reduce the client's sense of danger in our presence.

14. **Recurring crises signal problems in assessment or care.**

    What this means: We cannot blame our clients for recurring crises. When crises recur, we must identify factors contributing to it. When we work too fast and don't develop a comprehensive understanding of the current crisis, intervention plans may not be meaningful for the client. These plans are unlikely to work. Not all of those factors are within our or the client's control. When there are systemic barriers to appropriate care, we must help our clients overcome them as much as possible.

15. **Meaningful measures are taken to reduce the likelihood of future emergencies.**

    What this means: We must collaborate with the client to create a plan that will help overcome skills and resource deficits and systemic barriers to services. The more specific and collaborative an intervention and safety plan is, and the more frequently it is reviewed and adjusted to match new circumstances, the more likely it is to be effective.

Even in a crisis situation, your approach should be as collaborative as possible. James and Gilliland (2017, p. 90) differentiate between a "we" approach (collaborative) and an "I" approach (directive).

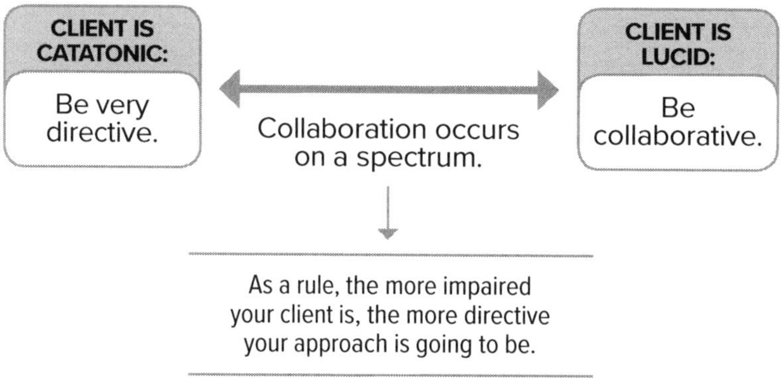

Figure 6

Here are two examples to illustrate:

Heather is a 24-year-old single woman with no social supports who struggles with addiction. She has called the crisis line stating that she wants to die today. You arrive at the home and notice that Heather is under the influence of substances. You determine that her thinking is erratic and delusional. In this case you are going to be *directive* in your approach. You are going to take action, because Heather can't make good decisions right now and is at risk of serious harm because of this.

Esperanza is a 22-year-old single mother of two young children. She called the crisis line today because she just can't cope and is thinking about taking all of her medications to end it all. When you arrive at the home, Esperanza is with her children. She is crying and expresses ambivalence about wanting to die. Her thinking is poor, but she is overwhelmed, not delusional. Esperanza hands you her medication, stating, "I want you to keep this for me." In this case you can be more collaborative in your approach. Esperanza is signaling that she is willing to collaborate. Keep in mind that Esperanza's state of mind could change and that you may need to move into a more directive approach.

Crisis Intervention Services: Parameters

> Crisis intervention services are always face-to-face and very short term.

By definition, crisis intervention services are *very short-term*. They end when the immediate mental health crisis ends. But, of course, service provision does not end. Here is an example:

Janelle has become more and more agitated over the past few weeks. She has struggled with depression for much of her life, but lately, it seems, things are getting worse. Janelle's partner of 2 years recently left her, stating that he just can't deal with her moods anymore. She has tried to cope by watching more television to distract herself and by drinking a bottle of wine to get to sleep at night. She now rarely leaves the house. Janelle sees a therapist once a week, but she is afraid to tell her therapist about her frequent suicidal thoughts, because she is afraid her therapist will put her in the "psych ward." She has been there and does not want to go back.

Today Janelle cannot stop thinking about suicide and finds herself in the kitchen holding a glass of water and a bottle of antidepressants. For a moment, she "wakes up" and she calls the local crisis line. The counselor is able to ascertain that Janelle has not taken any pills and keeps Janelle on the line until a crisis counselor arrives.

It is at this point that billable crisis intervention services begin, as the client is now seen face-to-face by a mental health professional.

The crisis counselor takes great care to be compassionate and to connect with Janelle in this very difficult situation. She understands that Janelle is frightened about being taken to a hospital against her will. She takes time to listen and understand Janelle's context, condition, and concerns. She assumes a nonthreatening posture and tone of voice while also asking, clearly, about Janelle's suicidal thoughts and plans. While doing so Janelle's counselor assesses:

- What initiated the crisis and how the Janelle is responding to it.
- Risk of lethality, violence, and any conditions, such as medical problems or substance abuse, contributing to the crisis.
- Janelle's mental status.
- Janelle's strengths, coping skills, and support network: The crisis counselor contacts Janelle's sister (with her permission) and she arrives to assist with planning to resolve the crisis.
- Service gaps that indicate additional treatment needs or care setting.

The crisis counselor also takes time to meet with Janelle's sister (with Janelle in sight) to further assess Janelle's needs and resources.

At this point Janelle and the crisis counselor determine together that Janelle does not want to die, but rather is overwhelmed and in desperate need of more intensive treatment and resources. She is looking for a "way out" and made an impulsive choice to pick up a bottle of pills. Had Janelle taken all of the pills in the bottle, she could easily have died. Janelle cannot quite explain how she got to the point of holding the bottle of pills in her hand. This is worrisome to the crisis counselor. It is clear that an airtight safety plan is needed. Because Janelle, at this point, denies wanting to die and having a plan to die, the crisis counselor determines that there is no need to call an ambulance and have Janelle transported to the hospital for an emergency psychiatric assessment.

Instead, Janelle and her crisis counselor, as well as Janelle's sister, sit down to create a crisis and safety plan together. A crisis plan accomplishes the following tasks:

- Deescalation of the crisis
- Client stabilization
- Restoration of safety (creating a client-centered and realistic safety plan)
- Appropriate referrals and linkages (Janelle's sister remains present, as it is assumed that Janelle cannot keep track of plans during this crisis)

Janelle, her sister, and the crisis counselor make the following plan and formalize this as a written safety plan that will become a part of the client's medical record:

1. Janelle will stay with her sister overnight. She will follow her safety plan. Janelle's sister will support her and intervene, if necessary, by calling 911 should Janelle become unsafe again.
2. Janelle's sister will sleep on the couch in Janelle's bedroom.
3. Janelle's sister will safeguard medication.
4. Janelle will participate in an intake appointment for an intensive outpatient program (IOP) the following day.
5. The crisis counselor will arrange for a next-day appointment with Janelle's psychiatric provider, following the IOP intake appointment. Because Janelle's psychiatric provider is a part of your agency provider network, she will have access to all of Janelle's records. Nevertheless, the crisis counselor sends an e-mail to Janelle's psychiatric provider to ensure that the provider is up to date about Janelle's increasing challenges.
6. Janelle will meet with her newly assigned TBS worker immediately following the IOP intake appointment. TBS will be provided daily until all resource needs are met.
7. Janelle will see her counselor within 2 days. TBS, counseling services, and pharmacological management services will coordinate their provision of care.
8. Janelle's counselor and TBS worker will explore the need for SUD services with Janelle.
9. Janelle makes a plan to attend the local NAMI depression support group on Saturday morning.

At the end of the crisis intervention service, Janelle is calmer. She is able to think, somewhat clearly, about the next few days. She explains that she will need lots of support. Janelle is still depressed but no longer in an acute crisis that requires ongoing crisis intervention.

Billable crisis intervention services for the acute mental health crisis have now concluded.

Does this mean that the crisis is over?

Take another look at crisis development:

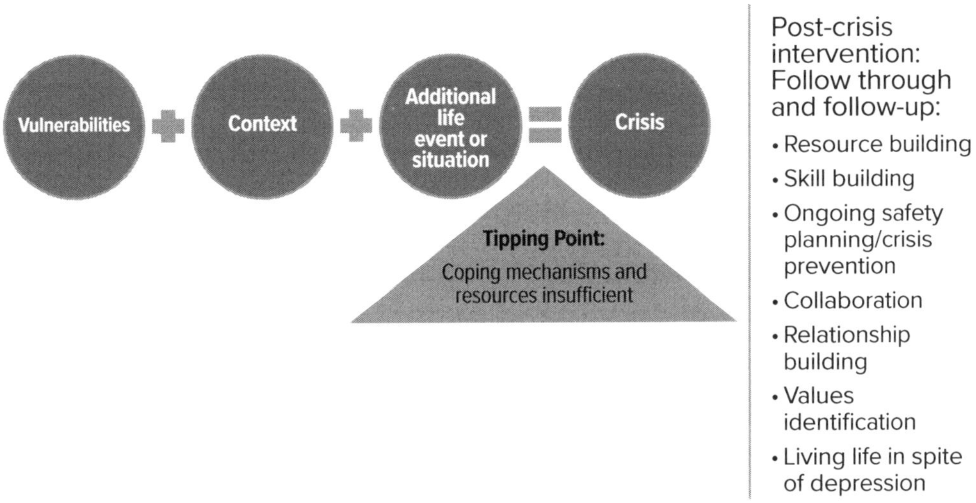

Figure 7

Post-crisis intervention services (after the immediate crisis has been alleviated and danger to self and others has passed) can take the shape of a wide range of services such as:

- Psychotherapy
- Therapeutic behavioral services (TBS)
- Community psychiatric supportive treatment (CPST)
- Intensive outpatient program (IOP)
- Medication management

Post-crisis intervention services are not billed as crisis intervention services. They follow the immediate mental health crisis. Post crisis intervention services can be longer-term services.

Peer support should also be arranged. Keep in mind that crises are intense and exhausting and that service plans should be realistic and collaboratively created. While it is often time to fill service gaps after a crisis, more services are not always better. Together you should choose the right kind of services at the right dosage to ensure your client is supported. Consider staggering new services one at a time to ensure your client does not view the very services that are meant to support her as a burden.

What about chronically suicidal clients?

Exposure to multiple ACEs can elevate the risk of suicidal thoughts and behaviors substantially. Those with exposure to childhood sexual abuse (CSA) can be especially at risk for chronic suicide risk (Jackson-Cherry & Erford, 2018, p. 161). For more information about ACEs and suicide risk, visit:

https://www.cdc.gov/violenceprevention/acestudy/index.html

We provide crisis intervention services when clients are at acute risk of serious harm to self and others. Chronic risk is by no means less dangerous and needs to be carefully monitored. When there is chronic, but not acute risk, we provide the full range of services to reduce risk, but not crisis intervention services. When we become aware of chronic risk, we move quickly into prevention mode:

- We may add and/or increase the intensity of services.
- We make a safety plan.
- We build resources.
- We work to increase client capacity to tolerate distress.
- We work to increase client ability to manage difficult emotions.
- We work to increase client relational connections.

Chronic risk "suggests the presence of longer-term potential of suicidality, but with less specificity of intent or plans (e.g., means and method) to carry out an attempt presently" (Jackson-Cherry & Erford, 2018, p. 161). Chronically suicidal clients need to be monitored carefully, because they can quickly move into an acutely suicidal state. When chronically suicidal clients move into an acutely suicidal state and risk of harm to self becomes imminent, crisis intervention services commence.

Here is an example of what this may look like:

Savannah is a 29-year-old woman with a history of CSA and a series of relationships that included domestic violence by a partner. Savannah struggles with depression, anxiety, and frequent anger outbursts but has been able to manage with the help of psychotherapy and medication. Savannah has also struggled with suicidal thoughts since the age of 13. She often thinks about ending her life, especially in stressful situations. Savannah is working with her therapist on managing these thoughts and has done well. She is able to work as a manager at a retail store and is currently in a committed and safe relationship.

Today Sarah's regional manager visited her store. He commented on her physical appearance and sexually harassed her in the back office. In response, Savannah punched him. There were no witnesses, and she was fired.

Savannah is distraught and dysregulated. She runs out of the store. Her thoughts of suicide intensify. She is flooded by memories of sexual abuse and feelings of worthlessness. She can no longer think clearly. She makes a plan to walk to a nearby highway and run into traffic. She calls her partner to say good-bye, but her partner manages to keep her on the phone until police arrive to transport her to the emergency room.

Savannah has reached her tipping point. The additional stressors of being sexually harassed and fired have rendered her coping mechanism insufficient. Savannah has moved into an acutely suicidal state.

Who Can Provide Crisis Intervention Services? How Are Specific Services Billed?

> Any provider of crisis intervention services must have a *current* certification in first aid and cardiopulmonary resuscitation (CPR) and must be trained in deescalation techniques.

Licensed practitioners can provide crisis intervention (both mental health and SUD) services in the form of crisis psychotherapy for clients who are known to them, but also for clients who are not known to them. In other words, they can be called into the community to assist a new client in a mental health crisis. This new client does not already have to be a client of the agency.

Psychotherapy for crisis is reported only once per day, and the total face-to-face time with the client and family is reported, even if the service was not continuous. The practitioner cannot provide services to other clients during crisis intervention.

Unlicensed practitioners can provide crisis intervention services, but only under the supervision of an independently licensed practitioner or physician/physician assistant who has recommended services, and only for clients who are currently on their caseload. Unlicensed practitioners cannot provide crisis psychotherapy, but they can provide crisis intervention services in the form of TBS and psychosocial rehabilitation (PSR) for crisis.

Care management specialists and peer recovery supporters cannot provide crisis intervention services.

When a current client is in crisis, *the most qualified available mental health provider should intervene*. If the client has a licensed therapist and the therapist is available to intervene right away, then the licensed therapist should provide crisis intervention services in the form of psychotherapy for crisis.

If a current client is in crisis and the licensed therapist is not available, the assigned community mental health worker should provide crisis intervention services in the form of TBS. When providing TBS in a crisis situation, check the "in crisis" box within the note to designate the service as a crisis service. If the community mental health worker determines that further assistance by a licensed therapist is needed, he must immediately notify his supervisor and the supervisor will assist with providing crisis intervention and/or ensuring that a licensed therapist is sent to assist right away.

If the assigned community mental health worker is not available to respond to the crisis in a timely manner, the therapist's and/or community mental health worker's supervisor must ensure that crisis intervention services are provided immediately by a qualified provider.

If we are called upon to provide crisis intervention for someone who is not yet a client, a licensed therapist must be the one to provide crisis intervention services.

The Need for a Crisis Intervention Model

Roberts and Ottens (2005) outline why a crisis intervention model is needed for practitioners responding to an acute mental health crisis. They explain that:

- Crises, by nature, are chaotic. A framework is needed to ensure order. For the practitioner, the crisis intervention model is this framework. The crisis intervention model keeps the practitioner on task and guards her from becoming absorbed in the intensity of the situation.
- A crisis intervention model can help the practitioner navigate between collaboration with the client and essential directive responses (such as calling 911 when the client's life is in danger) to avert harm to the client or others.
- The use of a crisis intervention model can ensure that all necessary steps are taken, including risk assessment, resource identification and referrals, and deescalation from crisis.

In summary, by following a crisis intervention model, the practitioner ensures that all of the client's needs are met in spite of very challenging circumstances.

Additionally, following a well-designed crisis intervention model provides protection for the practitioner. When using a crisis intervention model and documenting the use of such a model, the practitioner demonstrates that she is not haphazardly "winging it" when providing crisis intervention, but rather relying on a systematic and researched approach.

Adapting Roberts's Crisis Intervention Model

Roberts's seven-stage model (Roberts & Ottens, 2005) is well suited for crisis intervention services as defined by the State of Ohio, as most of it is focused on the sliver in time when the client is in an acute crisis. It also clearly delineates when the acute crisis ends and post-crisis intervention services, in the form of follow-up care, begin.

We have adapted Roberts's model to incorporate the importance of ongoing relationship building and co-regulation. The use of co-regulation as defined by Allan Schore (2008/2016) can be especially important in crisis intervention. When your client is in crisis, he cannot regulate his intense emotions of sadness, hopelessness, anger, rage, and shame. When you intervene, you will need to do so with a calm demeanor that signals safety, hope, connection and clarity. As you embody these qualities while providing crisis intervention services, you will communicate, both verbally and nonverbally, that safety can be built and intense feelings can be contained, accepted, and managed. Your demeanor often communicates more to that client than what you say (though your words are important, too).

Co-regulation happens when you attune with your client. This attunement is initially a right-brain-to-right-brain process, meaning it is nonverbal and intuitive. This process happens naturally, though you can intentionally initiate it. To engage in co-regulation, you need to perceive and connect with your client's state of mind, then use your well-regulated state of body and mind to help your client manage his. Your physical and emotional presence impacts the client's physical and emotional presence.

Think about co-regulation in the following way:

When you are upset, your client can sense this and may take it on. When you are calm, connected, and composed, your client can sense this, too, often without noticing. Communicating a calm, connected, and composed state of mind and body without words is the essence of co-regulation.

Co-regulation is about relationship. It is about truly getting to know, *in more than a cognitive way,* your client's state of mind and body. Co-regulation can be a critical tool when providing crisis intervention, as it can facilitate the process of deescalation and move the client from acute crisis , including an inability to connect with others and think rationally, into a more regulated state of mind in which verbal expression of needs and feelings can once again anchor the client in the context of human connections. In other words, co-regulation helps your client become present in the here and now. This here and now includes your helpful empathic presence.

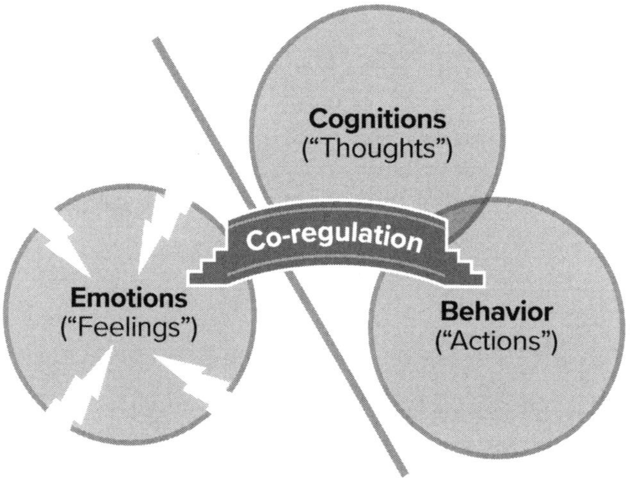

Emotions are intense. Client can't reflect. Client is stuck "feeling" and can't do anything else. Co-regulation can bridge the gap between client feelings and thoughts and actions.

Figure 8

When your client is in crisis, she is overwhelmed by intense emotions that drive irrational thoughts and harmful behavior. Co-regulation can calm those emotions, down-regulate the client's agitated state of body and mind, and return your client to the point where she can actually see you and others as helpful presences. The goal of co-regulation, ultimately, is to teach self-regulation. In a crisis situation, however, we are not concerned about immediately teaching self-regulation skills. Rather, we are concerned about returning the client to a somewhat regulated affective state in which she is able to think rationally again. Just the experience that affective states can change from completely dysregulated to somewhat calm in the presence of another human being is a helpful experience for your client.

The following figure represents our six-stage adaptation of Roberts's crisis intervention model:

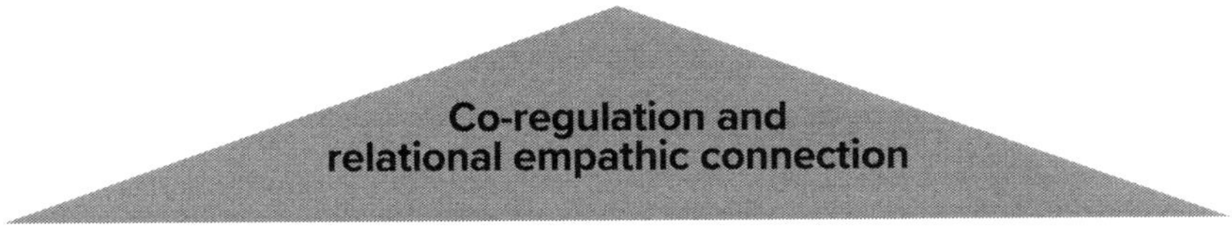

Six-Stage Crisis Intervention Model
1. Rapid assessment, including lethality assessment. *Billable crisis intervention services (face-to-face) begin.*
2. Identifying major problems or crisis precipitant: the tipping point.
3. Identifying feelings and emotions: active listening, validation, co-regulation, reframing.
4. Generating and exploring alternatives: connect and collaborate about plans.
5. Implementing an action plan: establish safety through agreed-upon means (can be removal of access to lethal means, hospitalization, supervision of client by parent, etc.). Beginning meaning making. *Billable crisis intervention services have concluded.*
6. Follow-up: post-crisis intervention

Figure 9

Roberts's original model contains seven stages of crisis intervention and designates relationship and rapport building as stage 2. Our adapted model looks at relationship and rapport building and the process of co-regulation as the "roof" under which all other stages take place. This adaptation of Roberts's model acknowledges that relationship and rapport-building are a part of every stage of the crisis model. The adaptation also acknowledges that crises are fluid and deescalation through relationship and co-regulation can become necessary again during any of the stages.

Think of this adapted model as a map for providing crisis intervention services. The map will ensure that you are walking in the right direction and not away from your destination.

Here is an example of how using our crisis intervention model can be helpful:

> Clinician Sarah arrives at the home of Allan, age 37, who is in crisis. He is thinking about overdosing on antidepressant medication, which is available to him right now. Sarah feels bad for Allan, who has a history of CSA. When she arrives, she helps him examine how the abuse he experienced as a child is contributing to his suicidal thoughts and plans. Allan expresses that he understands this. He cries while Sarah empathizes. Sarah agrees to see Allan again the following day. When she checks her phone the next morning, she finds a message that Allan has been hospitalized due to a suicide attempt (by overdose) that occurred several hours after Sarah left.

What went wrong?

- Sarah did not conduct a formalized suicide risk assessment, and did not know that Allan's risk was high and he was not able to commit to safety.
- Sarah focused her session on insight rather than assessment and safety planning. When a client is in crisis, insight is often limited and does not guarantee that suicide risk is lowered.
- Sarah did not connect Allan with additional resources or work on increasing coping skills for intense feelings. Neither Sarah nor Allan know what his coping skills are, or how they are lacking.
- Sarah did not make a plan to remove access to lethal means (his antidepressant medication). While it is impossible to remove all access to all lethal means (we cannot eliminate the presence of bridges to jump from), Sarah did not take the very important step of removing access to medications that could be lethal.

Had Sarah used our adapted crisis intervention model, she would have begun by building an empathic connection and then quickly moving into assessment of suicide risk. She would have documented her assessment, made a safety plan based on it, and arranged for appropriate post-crisis care.

This example also illustrates that crisis intervention services are different from other forms of psychotherapy. When there is imminent risk of harm to self or others, the provider needs to take charge and become directive. This does not mean that you should not collaborate with your client. You should collaborate with your client as much as possible during the crisis, but safety can never be secondary to collaboration. If your client wants to collaborate with you on a nonworkable safety plan, you must tell your client that the plan is nonworkable. If Allan had suggested putting his medications high on a shelf, Sarah would have needed to tell him that it was not a viable plan, because access was still possible.

As with any stage-based model, keep in mind that stages may need to be repeated and can overlap. Again, think of the model as a map or a guide. New roads can always be built, but you cannot function without a road map. Once you have become an experienced provider of crisis intervention services, the stages and components will become part of your internal GPS. You will know what you need to do without having to refer back explicitly to the crisis intervention model.

Walking Through the Stages of Crisis Intervention

Building the Roof

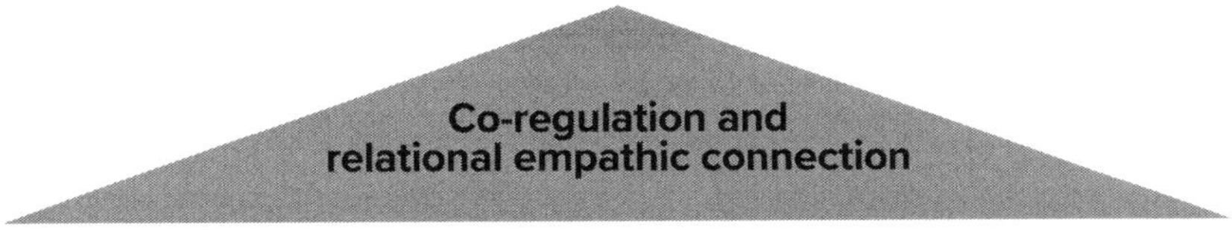

Figure 10

Before beginning the stages of crisis intervention, you must first build the "roof" under which those stages will take place. Carefully approach your client, but don't get too close. Use a soothing voice and assume a nonthreatening posture. Breathe calmly to regulate your own state of mind. Communicate verbally and nonverbally that you are here to help. Ask:

- *How can I help?*
- *What do you need?*
- *What can I do right now?*

If your client is willing to accept comfort items such as a stuffed animal, a fidget object, or a beautiful image, offer what is available. Ask if he would like to listen to soothing music or move to a more comfortable location. Your goal at this stage is simply to make a connection with your client and communicate that you are a safe person here to help.

Many of our clients have experienced trauma and toxic stress and can quickly slip into a fight-or-flight stance. Your client may perceive you as a threat, at least initially. You will need to work to overcome this perception. This can take time. Depending on what is needed, you may want to:

- Lower or raise the volume of your speech over time to see if your client can follow suit.
- Decrease or increase the speed of your speech.
- Slowly increase or decrease physical proximity to your client.
- Lower or speed up your breathing rate.

Do not rush through trying to build a connection. If your client gets a sense that you are rushed, you will seem far less safe to him. Listen empathically and with care. Validate your client's feelings without endorsing self-harm or harm to others. Be a soothing presence.

When your client can tolerate it and it is safe to do so, move a little closer. Check how your client responds. Ask about meaningful relationships, such as with partners, children, and pets. Wait for a facial expression that signals a connection, then focus the conversation on that connection. Embody what your client is looking for in meaningful relationships: acceptance, forgiveness, unconditional love. Let your client tell you more about those connections and the feelings associated with them.

Don't tell your client something like this:

- *It's not that bad.*
- *But you still have ________.*
- *At least you ________.*
- *But you are doing great.*

Comments like these can feel invalidating. If your client cannot talk about meaningful connections and denies having any, then build a meaningful connection right now. Be fully present. Be empathic. Validate. Co-regulate feelings and body states until your client is calmer.

This process of building an empathic and co-regulating relationship with your client in crisis will need to continue through all of the stages of intervention.

Keep in mind that when your client is in crisis, it is unlikely that she can think clearly. In all likelihood she is stuck in right-brain processes focused on anger, rage, and shame. Jackson-Cherry & Erford (2018, p. 177) refer to the state of mind of a suicidal client as a "'brain condition' with cognitive distortions and perception and proportion difficulties." Don't assume that your client can think clearly, or think much at all.

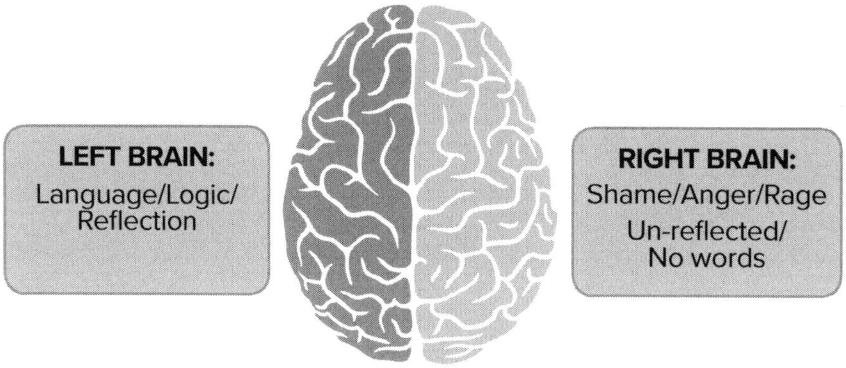

Figure 11

These kinds of processes do not respond well to language-based interventions, but they do respond to nonverbal co-regulatory interventions using:

- Calm breathing
- Soothing tone of voice
- Nonthreatening posture
- Friendly gestures

- Soothing sounds
- Soothing spaces
- Soothing items
- Soothing people

It's OK to use words, but it's also important to understand that *your demeanor and actions* are likely far more important than what you say. Once your client has made a connection with you, you can slowly move into language.

Now you are ready to proceed to the six stages of our model.

1. Building the House: Rapid Assessment, Including Assessment of Risk of Harm to Self and Others

> Never put your life at risk when providing crisis intervention services. If a dangerous weapon is present and your client threatens you or herself, call 911 and do not approach.

We are frequently called to assist when our clients engage in nonsuicidal self-injury (NSSI). NSSI is often very distressing to those who are close to the person who self-injures. However, it serves a very different purpose than suicidal plans and behaviors. Peterson, Freedenthal, Sheldon, and Andersen (2008) explain that NSSI:

- is a tool to cope with intense affective states;
- is used to lower emotional distress or step away from it;
- occurs in the context of many emotional disorders, such as depression and anxiety; and
- is not meant to result in death.

Because there is no imminent risk of serious harm or death, the occurrence of an NSSI event by itself does not call for crisis interventions. Of course, clients who engage in NSSI should receive the full range of appropriate services, including psychotherapy, TBS, medication management services, IOP, and any other supportive service. Clearly, clients who self-injure need to learn to accept, sit with, tolerate, and manage intense affective states.

When you are meeting with a client who engages in NSSI, you must ask questions like this:

- *When you are doing this (cutting/burning yourself, etc.), is there any part of you that wants you die, perhaps even just by accident?*
- *Is there even just a little part of you that wants to end your life when you are doing this?*

If your client denies this (and you will have to reassess often), then she should be assessed as engaging in NSSI. If your client endorses that even just a small part of her hopes the NSSI could lead to her death, then she is moving into suicidal behavior, and her self-injury needs to be classified as a suicide attempt.

It is important to note that "a growing body of literature suggests that NSSI may be an especially important risk factor for suicidal behavior" (Klonsky, Victor, & Saffer, 2014, p. 566). This makes sense when you think of emotional distress and self-injurious behavior occurring on a spectrum:

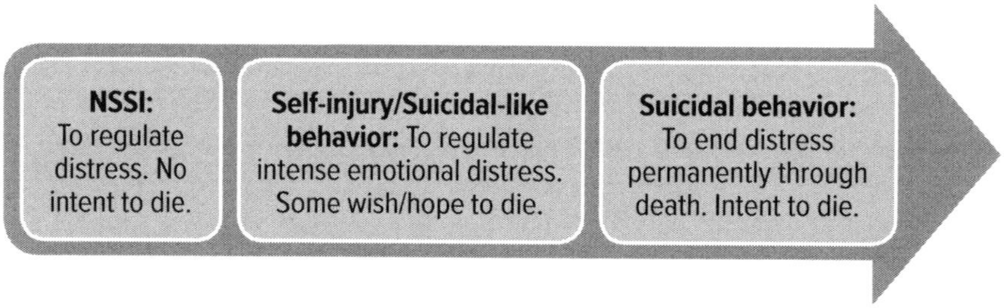

Figure 12

What this means for our clients is that:

- We provide a wide range of services for clients who engage in NSSI (but not crisis intervention services).
- We must frequently monitor if a client is moving toward self-injury with some hope or intent to die.

We provide crisis intervention services at the point at which the client who is engaging in self-injurious behaviors endorses at least some intent or hope to die, and there is imminent risk of serious harm or death.

Additionally, we must always assess how potentially lethal a client's NSSI is. Clients may engage in behaviors that are not intended to result in death, but could. When this is the case, crisis intervention services are in order, because the client is at imminent risk of serious harm or death, even if she is not aware of the risk.

Suicide Rates and Risk

Suicide is one of the leading causes of death in the United States. According to the Centers for Disease Control and Prevention (CDC; 2018a), suicide rates rose more than 30% in nearly half of the states between 1999 and 2016, including a 36% increase for Ohio. Data from the newest Youth Risk Behavior Survey (CDC, 2018b), conducted by the CDC, shows that nearly 14% of high school students—and 17% of teen girls—have made a plan for completing suicide.

These numbers serve as a sobering reminder of the need to always assess for suicide risk. Fifty-five percent of our clients have had exposure to at least four ACEs, meaning that we serve a population whose suicide risk is higher than average.

> Suicide risk assessment must be a part of any mental health assessment and suicide risk must be addressed with the full range of services available and appropriate to decrease risk. Suicide prevention is especially important in community mental health, because many of our clients are at a higher risk of suicide.

Assessing for Risk of Harm to Self

Rapid assessment begins as soon as you are face-to-face with your client. Before you arrive on the scene, you may be able to access information about your client using the electronic client record to aid in your assessment. Still, every crisis requires a full assessment of the current situation, including current crisis triggers. Do not assume that your client is not a risk to herself because she has made vague suicidal gestures in the past and has never followed through.

When you arrive, take a quick look around. Determine if it is safe for you to approach your client. If your client is holding a weapon of any kind, do not approach.

- If the "weapon" is a pencil and your client is a 9-year-old child, calmly speak with the child from a safe distance until he puts the pencil down and you can safely approach.
- If your client is a 16-year-old young man who is holding a knife or a gun, step away and call 911, explaining that your client who is struggling with mental illness has a weapon and you need immediate assistance. Crisis intervention services are not meant to put your life at risk. Wait until safety forces arrive and the situation is under control.

If you can safely approach, make contact with your client using all of your co-regulatory skills and strategies. Once you have made a meaningful connection, ask short, simple questions about the situation. You want to understand how the following components relate to the development of the crisis:

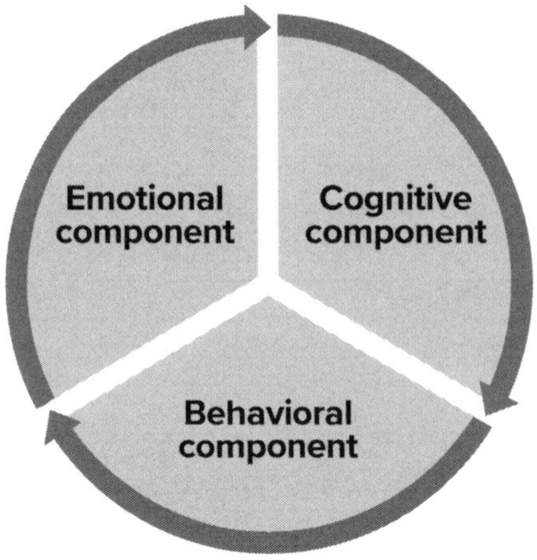

Figure 13

Roberts and Ottens (2005, p. 324) point out that "ascertaining whether the client has actually initiated a suicide attempt, such as ingesting poison or an overdose of medication," is of the utmost importance. Begin your assessment by asking:

- ***Have you taken anything or done anything today to end your life?***
- ***Have you taken any drugs today that could accidentally end your life, even if you did not mean to end your life?***

If you find that your client has taken a dangerous substance (pills, bleach, etc.) or has substantially injured herself (other than superficial self-harm such as scratches on the surface of the skin), immediately call 911. If necessary, provide CPR after you call 911 and follow instructions from the 911 operator.

If your client denies that a suicide attempt is in progress, use the Columbia Lighthouse Project Columbia-Suicide Severity Rating Scale (C-SSRS) to assess for suicidal thoughts, plans, and intent. The C-SSRS addresses all three components outlined in the nearby image. Additionally, it is important to understand "that a structured assessment of suicidal ideation and behavior significantly improves identification of high-risk patients relative to a routine clinical interview" (Yeager & Roberts, 2015, pp. 47–48). In the heat of the moment it is easy to forget to ask a question or to complete a component of the assessment. Empathy pulls us in the direction of wanting to help as quickly as possible. But in order to be truly helpful, we must understand the suicidal crisis not just empathically, but also analytically. The use of the C-SSRS can help us stay on track and learn as much as we can about the complex situation of a suicidal crisis.

You can find the C-SSRS (or Columbia Scale) embedded in the electronic client record. If you do not have access, you can find it on the Columbia Lighthouse Project website.

Using this scale will help you ask the right kinds of questions in the right way. This is especially important if you are not yet comfortable asking difficult questions. Additionally, the Columbia Scale is well researched. You can find more information about this research on the Columbia Lighthouse Project website.

The scale is available in multiple languages, and there is a version for very young children. Suicide risk assessment for very young children requires parental or caretaker involvement. It can be difficult for parents and caretakers to acknowledge that a child is having suicidal thoughts, plans, and intent. The C-SSRS for children can assist with finding words to ask the right kinds of questions to children and their caretakers. When a child is suicidal, the child's parent or caretaker can play a crucial role in helping the child stay safe by securing the environment and providing supervision.

Keep in mind that it can be difficult or impossible for a parent (especially a single parent) to constantly supervise a suicidal child. When a child is in a prolonged suicidal crisis, the parent needs support. Hospitalizations can add additional trauma to the client's life but cannot always be avoided. Systemic barriers to appropriate care for children in a suicidal crisis include the lack of supportive services for the parent. Parents who care for a suicidal child may lose income and employment as a consequence. A wider range of hospitalization settings that acknowledge the need to step children down into less restrictive settings as quickly as possible, while still providing a secure and supervised setting, needs to be developed and funded.

> Always carry a paper copy of the Columbia Scale with you in case you do not have internet connectivity. Always document that you have used the Columbia Scale to assess for suicide risk and the outcome of the assessment.

Once you have completed the suicide risk assessment, you will need to take action based on the outcome of the assessment. Before you do so, keep in mind that no assessment tool has been found to accurately predict whether or not a client will attempt suicide. This makes sense for the following reasons:

Clients may not be truthful when answering questions about suicidal thoughts, plans, and intent, or may feel conflicted and be unable to articulate complex thoughts and feelings about suicide.

The determination of whether a client needs an emergency psychiatric assessment cannot be made solely on the basis of the outcome of a rating scale. If necessary, consult with a supervisor.

Jackson-Cherry & Erford (2018, p. 172) point out the need to use more than one form of assessment and gather as much collateral information as possible. This means that you will need to:

- Use the C-SSRS and have a conversation with your client. Your client may tell you something in an informal conversation that she is not willing to tell when you are using a rating scale.
- Gather information (with client permission) from collaterals such as spouses, parents, and partners. This is especially important if your client cannot think

clearly during the crisis. Others may be able to provide clinically important information.

You will need to use your clinical judgment about risk, taking into account all of the factors you have come to know, including the client's resilience. Ask:

- *What keeps you from killing yourself?*
- *Who keeps you from killing yourself?*
- *What do you have to look forward to?*
- *How well are you supported?*

Community Mental Health Alert

More than half of our clients (55%) have had four or more adverse childhood experiences (ACEs). This puts them at a much higher risk for mental illness. Merrick et al. (2017) noted that the risk of attempting suicide increases exponentially for those who have six or more ACEs.

If your assessment points to the need for an emergency psychiatric assessment, your client will need to be transported to the ER. Because you have determined that your client is at imminent risk for self-harm, you cannot transport your client. Call an ambulance.

If your assessment has determined that your client is not at imminent risk for suicide (does not have a plan and means), you will need to develop a safety plan with your client (see stage 5 of our crisis intervention model).

Assessing Risk of Harm to Others

When a client makes a credible threat to seriously hurt or kill another person or persons, you must, as quickly as possible, contact your supervisor to aid in decision making about client care and determination of r isk.

Sometimes clients make threats to seriously harm or kill others. These threats must always be taken seriously and assessed—even when your client is a child or adolescent. Not every threat, however, triggers a duty to protect (a formal process written into Ohio's laws and rules).

Thoughts of violent revenge are not uncommon, and to a certain degree, they are normal. Our clients may refer to wanting to kill a person who has hurt them (or a family member), but they are really just using this language to vent intense emotions. They are trying to cope. When clients make specific threats about seriously hurting or killing another person, we must then assess if they truly mean to carry out their threats (Jackson-Cherry & Erford, 2018, p. 181). When a threat is made, we must ask:

1. ***What do you mean by that?***
2. ***If you think about this clearly, do you really want to kill this person?***
3. ***Have you thought about how you would kill this person?***
4. ***Do you have a plan to kill this person?***
5. ***Do you have access to the means you need to kill this person?***

This assessment mimics the suicide risk assessment. It is important to thoroughly explore answers to questions 1 and 2. If you determine that your client does not really mean to kill the other person, but rather is using violent threats as a means to cope, you can then:

- Validate your client's intense feelings behind the threat, but not the threat itself.
- Help your client understand potential implications, including legal consequences, of making violent threats. Do this compassionately. Explain that you want to ensure that your client does not have the additional burden of legal troubles. When a child or adolescent makes a threat, you must contact the parent or guardian to ensure they can assist with keeping the child and everyone else safe. Explain to the parent that you are trying to protect the child from choices with serious negative consequences.
- Help your client identify more adaptive ways of coping with intense feelings.

Be sure to validate intense feelings, but never endorse violence as a legitimate way to manage them.

Use a well-researched and validated assessment tool to complete your formalized assessment of risk to others. Those at OhioGuidestone should use the Risk Assessment for Violence form, which can be found on the OhioGuidestone intranet, on the Clinical Documents page. Those outside of OhioGuidestone must follow their agency's protocols and procedures regarding a risk assessment for violence.

If it becomes clear that your client intends to carry out a plan to seriously harm or kill another person, or to target a specific location such as a school, you are legally required to take measures to protect potential victims. Ohio duty to protect laws and rules apply. Familiarize yourself with the laws and rules, and work with your supervisor to determine how they apply to you and to specific situations you may encounter. You can review Ohio's duty to protect laws and rules here: http://codes.ohio.gov/oac/5122-3-12

The following outlines OhioGuidestone's procedure for addressing threats of serious harm to others. Anyone providing mental health services at OhioGuidestone, including nonlicensed providers, must follow this procedure. Please note that the procedures outlined below require very specific steps, such as notifying local police and all potential victims (or their parents) of a credible threat. No providers should manage the situation of a credible client threat alone. Your supervisor must be notified promptly so you can work together on ensuring everyone's safety.

Sometimes children make alarming threats to hurt others but do not have intent or means to carry them out. Here is an example:

> Jose is a 6-year-old learning-disabled student who struggles with depression and anxiety. He has experienced significant trauma, including physical and sexual abuse, and often responds with physical aggression to any threat, perceived or real. Today, Jose is struggling with classwork. He becomes agitated and runs out of his classroom. When a teacher stops him in the hallway, he kicks her. The school's crisis intervention team arrives and restrains Jose, then transports him to an empty classroom to help him cool down. Jose becomes panicked and begins throwing chairs and other items. He is restrained again. At this point, Jose's fight response overrides his ability to think clearly and he screams: "I am going to kill you! I am going to kill you all!"

Should you consider this a serious and credible threat?

Jose's behavior is out of control and he is making this threat while physically restrained. At this point, this is not a credible threat. You should wait until Jose is calmer and better able to think. At that point you can assess if Jose has the plan, intent, and means to carry out his threat. Because he made the threat in a very agitated state, it is quite possible that he does not even remember it. In all likelihood Jose does not actually want to harm his teachers and classmates, but rather was overwhelmed and in a neurobiological state of "fight." His words were a reflection of his state of mind rather than an expression of actual intent.

At what point should you be concerned about Jose? You should be concerned if:

- He continues to make threats to kill, even when deescalated.
- He makes references to using a lethal weapon such as a gun or sharp object.
- He explains where he could find a lethal weapon or hints at having access to one.
- His parents make light of his threats and are unwilling to secure weapons in the home.
- He intentionally sets a fire.
- He intentionally seriously hurts an animal.
- Your clinical judgment tells you that he poses a serious threat of harm to others (notify your supervisor and discuss the situation together).

It is better to err on the side of caution. Always consult with your supervisor if your clinical judgment tells you that someone, even a young child, may carry out a threat.

If your client is a child and guns are not properly secured in the home, and the parent or caretaker refuses to secure them, a call to a child abuse hotline may be warranted, because the parent is putting the child at risk by permitting access to firearms. It is always preferable to make a plan with the parent to move firearms out of the home for the time being. Be sure to explain, if needed, that you are in no way questioning the parent's right to own a firearm, but rather that you are acting out of concern for everyone's safety, including the safety of your client and all family members.

If your client is an adult, help the adult make a decision to remove access to guns. Again, explain that you are taking this step to protect your client from doing harm. Locking a gun in a safe is not enough. The firearm must be moved out to another location where it is safely locked away in a proper gun safe (to which your client does not have access).

The following procedures must be followed in the event that an OhioGuidestone staff person becomes aware, either directly or through a knowledgeable person, of a threat of harm made by an OhioGuidestone client:

Immediate and Emergent Threats

If the staff member believes the client is expressing a credible threat that could cause serious immediate and emergent physical harm or death, the staff should contact law enforcement (call 911) immediately and follow all directives. Once emergency responders have been notified, staff should proceed with step 2.1.

Non-Emergent Threats

1. In all other circumstances, the staff must gather all information necessary to assess the following:
    a. Whether the client has the intent to carry out the threat;
    b. Whether the client has the ability to carry out the threat;
    c. Whether the threat is an explicit threat of inflicting imminent and serious physical harm or death; and
    d. Whether the threat is made toward a clearly identifiable victim, which includes a threat to a readily identifiable structure and potential occupants of the structure (e.g., a threat to a school).
2. **The staff should immediately contact a supervisor to make a determination as to whether the above criteria have been met.** If there are questions regarding whether the criteria in 2.1 are met, the supervisor should contact the program director to make the final determination.
3. If the supervisor determines that the criteria in 2.1 ARE met, the supervisor will direct staff to follow one or more of the actions (2.3.1–2.3.3) below and then to continue with steps 2.3.4 and 2.3.5:
    a. Initiate efforts to hospitalize the client on a voluntary basis.
    b. Initiate efforts to hospitalize the client on an involuntary (emergency) basis.
    c. Develop or review and update a safety plan that is reasonably calculated to eliminate the possibility that the client will carry out the threat.
        i. This safety plan MUST be approved by a supervisor (in person or by phone) before concluding the appointment and be filed in the electronic client record within 24 hours of incident.

ii. Review the Individual Treatment Plan as necessary.

d. Communicate to a law enforcement agency in the area where each potential victim resides, where the threatened structure is located, or where the client or patient resides, and if feasible, communicate to each potential victim or a potential victim's parent or guardian if the potential victim is a minor all of the following information:
   i. Nature of the threat;
   ii. The identity of the client making the threat (including contact information and address); and
   iii. The identity of each potential victim of the threat (including any contact information and address, if known).

e. Complete the Duty to Protect Report and document the situation in a progress note. Duty to Protect Report (and any assessment tools utilized relating to the incident) shall be filed in the electronic client record under the Documents tab.
   i. Complete the electronic Internal Risk Incident Report within 24 hours of incident.
   ii. If client information is reported outside the agency to a law enforcement agency (or another third party), staff will complete the "Documentation of Disclosures of Protected Health Information" form which is located in the client record.

4. If the situation does NOT meet the criteria in #2, staff shall take the following actions:
   a. Complete the Duty to Protect Report (and document the reasons why the situations did not warrant a Duty to Protect response) and document the situation in a progress note. Duty to Protect Report (and any assessment tools utilized relating to the incident) shall be filed in the electronic client record under the Documents tab.
   b. Create, review, and/or update a safety plan as necessary to address any concerns identified. Review the Individual Treatment Plan as needed.

Related Documents:

- Duty to Protect Form (available on the intranet)
- Internal Risk Incident Report (electronic)
- Documentation of Disclosures of Protected Health Information (electronic)
- Related assessment tools (e.g., Risk Assessment of Violence, Lethality Tool, Columbia-Suicide Severity Rating Scale [C-SSRS]).

These procedures are here to assist you with proper decision making and following the law. Additionally, as outlined in the procedure, you must document what you have done in the client file and complete additional forms and documentation as outlined. If you don't document what you have done, legally, it "did not happen."

Complete all of your documentation concurrently or, when this is not possible due to the level of crisis, within 24 hours of service.

2. Identification of Major Problems or Crisis Precipitant: the Tipping Point

Ask: "What happened? Why now?" You are looking for the tipping point. If you can identify what led to an acute crisis, you can begin to formulate a plan to resolve it.

Every crisis is different. You will have to discern what led to it. When you are doing so, you are not working on helping your client develop a deep understanding her difficulties; she is in crisis and cannot think clearly. Additionally, exploring past hurts in depth while in crisis could actually make things worse. You are looking to deescalate the crisis and help your client to move away, step by step, from thoughts, feelings, and behaviors that put her at risk for harm to self and others.

Nevertheless, how you ask your questions matters. Roberts and Ottens (2005, p. 334) reference an "artful interviewing style that allows this information to emerge as the client's story unfolds." Here are some do's and don'ts:

Don't:

- Demand answers.
- Ask lengthy, complicated questions.
- Rush through things.
- Suggest specific answers.
- Hint that one answer is better than another.
- Arrive at quick and simple conclusions without evidence.
- Forget about your co-regulation skills.
- Become impatient or agitated.
- Suggest that you know better than your client.

Do:

- Continue to connect with your client using empathy and co-regulation.
- Listen carefully.
- Clarify answers using follow-up questions.
- Allow your client to take time for thinking and answering. Tolerate silence for a while.
- Accept answers you don't completely understand yet.

- Ask about timing: Why now?
- Regulate your own state of body and mind continuously.
- Accept your client as a valid source of information.
- Collect information from collaterals.
- Begin to conceptualize how the client arrived at her tipping point using the information she is giving you.

Remember, your goal at this stage is to understand why the client is in acute crisis now. You are trying to understand why coping skills and resources that were at least marginally sufficient yesterday are no longer sufficient today.

Here are things you can say and some questions you can ask at this stage:

- *It sounds like today everything just became too much.*
- *Tell me more about what happened today/yesterday?*
- *Who did you meet yesterday/today?*
- *Who walked away from you?*
- *What made things so much worse for you?*
- *What did somebody say to you that made things worse for you?*
- *What did somebody say about you that made things worse for you?*
- *What did you come to believe that is making things worse for you today?*

> Be sure to alternate questions with empathic statements and actions. Otherwise your client may feel like he is being "interrogated," and this may put him into a defensive (fight/flight) state.

Once you have a working model of what may have led to the acute crisis, ask your client about it. Start with: *Here is what I am thinking may have happened.* Explain your conceptualization, then ask: *Am I getting this right?*

If you didn't get it right, gather more information and use this time to connect empathically with your client.

3. Identification of Feelings and Emotions: Active Listening, Validation, Co-regulation, Reframing

> You have two tasks at this stage:
> You are listening, validating, and co-regulating.

You are also beginning help your client deescalate by gently introducing alternative behavioral choices for managing intense feelings.

Your client is in the midst of an acute crisis. She is overwhelmed by intense emotions and struggles to understand them. Think of her emotions as a boiling pot on the stove:

Figure 14

The first order of business is to turn off the stove. You can do this by:

- Using co-regulation to calm intense states of body and mind.
- Reflective listening.
- Validating feelings, but not endorsing violence toward self and others.
- Using the senses to bring your client back into the room, away from anger, rage, and shame. You can ask your client to smell a flower, an orange, or perfume, or bite into a piece of chocolate or take a sip of lemonade (use a paper cup). You can ask permission to play soothing music. You can hand your client a soothing item. If your client can tolerate the presence of a soothing person, such as a partner or parent, this can also be helpful.

Next, you are going to help your client identify and be able to give a name to the multitude of feelings she is experiencing. Naming a feeling "conquers" it. Keep it simple. Your client is still in the midst of an acute crisis. This is not the time for your client to differentiate between indignation and resentment. Rather, you want to give the basic feelings you see in front of you a name. You can ask:

- *What you are describing sounds like rage to me. Am I getting this right?*
- *It sounds like you are feeling unworthy. Is that what you are feeling?*
- *Are you feeling that you are sad? Bad? Like a bad person?*
- *I am wondering if you are feeling desperate, like there is no way out. Is that what you are feeling?*

- *I hear you talking about how bad the future looks to you right now. Are you feeling hopeless?*

Once you have identified two or three major feelings, summarize what your client has told you. Then normalize those feelings without devaluing them. This can sound something like this:

> *We have been talking for a while and it sounds like you have all kinds of overwhelming feelings going on right now. You have told me about feeling hopeless and ashamed [give examples]. These kinds of feelings are difficult to have and to share. I am so glad we were able to take a look at those feelings and give them a name. That's a great step. You are in a tough spot. Just know that others have been there before. You are not alone. It can get better. You don't have to do this alone. I am here to help. I understand that this is not easy.*

So far you have validated and named feelings. Now it is time to begin to "feel out" how you can help your client turn toward better ways of coping. That's not easy. Your task is to be validating and point toward the possibility of change at the same time.

You can think of your task in the following way:

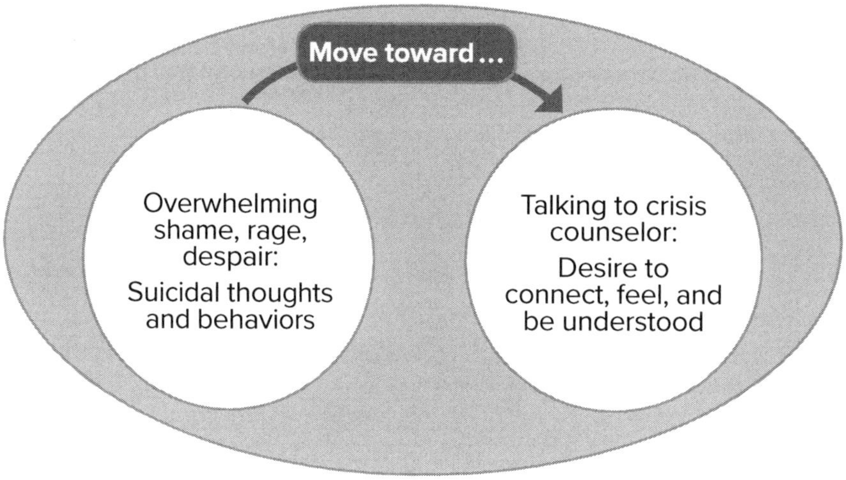

The client's reality is contained in the large oval. She is focused on the left side of the oval, yet, she is talking to you. Your job is to simply help her turn toward her desire to connect and feel and be understood without denying her feelings of shame, rage, and despair.

Figure 15

In order for your client to turn toward her desire to connect and feel understood, you will need to continue to help her regulate her state of body and mind, using co-regulation and connection strategies that involve the senses.

When you gently help your client move toward acknowledging her desire for connection, you are preparing her to explore specific alternatives to suicide. This can sound something like:

- *You have told me about your despair and hopelessness. And that it seems that there is no way out for you. I am wondering how you feel about connecting with me. Is it possible that, just for a moment, you felt connected with me? If you did, is it possible that there are others who want to connect with you? I am wondering about [name important person or pet].*
- *You have told me how you feel about [name]. I am wondering if there's a way you could continue to be a part of this person's life. When you talk about _________ your face lights up just a bit. This sounds important to you. Perhaps it can continue to be important.*
- *You have told me about [meaningful activity]. When you talk about this thing that you do, your face lights up just a bit, almost as if you enjoyed the activity. I am wondering if there could be more of this in your life.*

You get the idea. You are not trying to tell your client that she should not feel the way she does; you are saying that there may be another way to look at life, one that would keep her alive and connected.

If your client can't move toward the idea of connection and meaning, continue to assess. Listen. Co-regulate. Be patient. Sometimes clients are not able to make life-affirming decisions. This is not your fault. When your client is unable to move toward connection and safety, it is time to become more directive and initiate a possible hospitalization.

4. Generate and Explore Alternatives: Connect and Collaborate About Plans

> Be inclusive of and appreciative of diverse backgrounds when helping your client generate alternatives to suicidal behavior. Don't dismiss a suggestion your client makes just because you are unfamiliar with the client's cultural heritage. Ask questions. Then listen for "gems" in your client's words and use those gems to help your client paint a picture of his life in which he is important, valued, and loved.

At this point your client should have regained a basic ability to think. You have helped him sort through and name his emotions. You are now trying to establish what needs to happen next. Think of this stage as a crossroads. You are helping your client determine which way he needs to go.

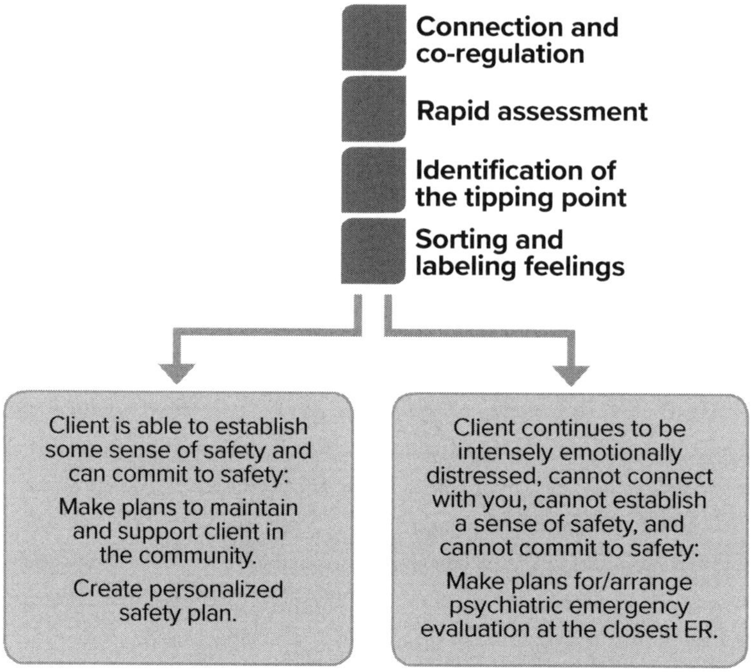

Figure 16

Your primary objective at this stage is to help your client explore alternatives to suicide. Any plan you make is likely to be effective only if your client plays a significant role in identifying alternatives to suicide. Telling your client what he should do instead of committing suicide is not effective. But keep in mind that your client's thought processes may be slow and limited. You can help by asking questions or providing suggestions:

- *How are you feeling about creating safety right now?*
- *What do you think it would take for you to be safe?*
- *What kinds of supports do you need?*
- *Who could help?*
- *Where would you feel safer?*
- *What makes you feel safer?*

> Meaningful interpersonal connections are the most effective way to build safety. Look for those connections in your client's life and help him recognize them.

Because your client may struggle with thinking, you may want to make suggestions about creating safety. Keep in mind that you cannot "push" your client into safety. Sometimes clients agree to safety plans or suggestions about how to stay safe to please us or to simply get us to leave. When this happens, the client remains at risk for suicide. Always ask: How can we make this fit you? What would make this *your* plan?

Here are some suggestions you may want to make:

- Removing access to lethal means for suicide
- Staying with a loved one or friend
- Learning how to use self-soothing
- Attending day treatment/intensive outpatient treatment (IOP)
- Learning about or taking medication to manage mood
- Helping others
- Becoming physically active
- Creating a safety network
- Attending support groups
- Asking for help
- Building a life around value-based actions

The measures that you put in place with your client have to be right for the situation. If your client struggles with intense thoughts of suicide, giving him a stress ball to squeeze is not in any way sufficient. If you can, involve collaterals in the identification of measures that can be put in place. Parents and spouses or partners often know what will help. Keep in mind that the roles of children, parents, and spouses are often culturally prescribed. Be respectful of your client's cultural contexts, but also acknowledge and respect any need your client may have to step outside of culturally prescribed roles.

If you can generate alternatives to suicide, you can move forward and begin to make a formalized safety plan. Additionally, it's important to help your client move toward hope for a better life. Many clients will ask *why* they should stay alive. When this happens, help your client explore:

- What is important to him.
- Who is important to him.
- Changes he would like to see in his world and how he could help make these changes happen. Keep it simple, small, and local.

Help your client paint a picture of his world in which he is important, valued, and loved. Spend some time bringing the picture to life using her words. In this way you can be inclusive of your client's entire context, including his cultural background. But remember that culture can create restrictions and demands that become burdensome. If your client feels restricted and burdened by cultural expectations, and this contributes to his suicidal thoughts and behavior, be clear about recognizing this and help him think about ways in which he can step out of his context. Here are some examples:

- A 17-year-old Puerto Rican high school student is told by his family that he can't be gay. His mother asks her Pentecostal minister to come to the home to cast out "the demon of homosexuality." The student loves his family, including his mother, but feels hopeless about his future and ever being able to be himself.
- An 18-year-old immigrant from Somalia who came to the United States as a refugee with her family is about to enter an arranged marriage. She wants to finish high school and go to college but is expected to take care of her siblings until she is married and have children and tend to the home after her marriage. She feels that her life is over.
- A 47-year-old Caucasian factory worker is laid off. He is now unable to provide for his family. He feels overwhelmed by expectations to be a provider and hopeless about his chances to ever find a job again. Self-sufficiency has always been important to him, and now he feels like a failure.

5. Implementing the Action Plan: Making Safety Possible

> Create a road map with your client to get to and maintain safety. This road map takes the form of a safety plan. Safety plans must be collaboratively created and highly personalized. They must have the highest possible degree of specificity in order to be effective. They should be reviewed and amended frequently to incorporate changes in the client's life and ability to cope. And they must be discontinued when they are no longer needed.

Once you have explored alternatives to suicide with your client, you are ready to take a step forward to determine which direction your client needs to take:

Figure 17

If your client cannot commit to safety in a meaningful way, or your clinical judgment tells you that she just appeasing you, you must initiate an emergency psychiatric assessment at the closest ER. Do not transport the client, as this poses a risk to both of you. Call an ambulance or ask a parent, partner, spouse or friend to call.

HIPAA allows you to provide PHI (protected health information) that is necessary for the assessment and treatment of your client in the emergency room without an additional release of information. Disclosure to ensure continuity of care is covered in our initial consent for treatment. Disclose only what is needed to provide appropriate care.

The emergency psychiatric assessment may determine that your client is not at risk for suicide and send her home. When this happens, your client will need timely follow-up services (no longer billed as crisis intervention services). When you meet with your client after an ER visit, you must reassess for risk of harm to self and others, and then move into safety planning. Risk can change quickly, especially for clients who struggle with distress tolerance. Teaching clients affect regulation and distress-tolerance skills after a visit to the ER and/or a hospitalization is vitally important.

If your client is willing and able to establish a sense of safety and she is able to maintain this sense of and commitment to basic safety while you are meeting with her, then you are ready to create a formalized road map with her to help her create and maintain safety. This formalized road map takes the shape of a safety plan. Safety plans can be meaningful and effective if they are highly personalized and created collaboratively. All too often, however, they look like generic plans, and it seems like they were created to fulfill a requirement rather than to be used as a meaningful tool. Here is an example from an ineffective safety plan:

Behavior of Concern: Client is angry.
Supports to Assist: Mom
Coping Skills to Use: All available skills.

Note the lack of specificity. We do not know why the client is angry or how he expresses his anger in ways that are not safe. We know that Mom is a source of support, but there is no cell phone number noted, nor is there a backup plan for when Mom can't be reached or does not know how to help. Coping skills are not spelled out, and we do not know if the client is able to effectively use them. In all likelihood, current coping skills were not sufficient.

The following is an example of an effective safety plan:

Safety Plan
Please select AND describe one of the below: ☐ **Specific Behavior/Increased Symptom/Decreased Functionality:** Jose picks up butter knives and threatens to stab his mother ☐ **Other Problem or Concern:** Jose is diagnosed with ADHD, does not always take his medication. Jose's father was murdered 6 months ago.
Client Name: Jose Sample
DOB: 6/22/2013
Program: School Services
Date: 6/22/18

Safety Plan (continued)			
What steps have been taken to make sure the client is safe? Jose's mother has taken all knives from the kitchen and secured them in a lockbox. She carries the key on her person at all times. Jose's mother has removed sharp objects from his room. They are locked in the garage.			
Please describe the signs or indicators that a crisis is developing for the client. Include thoughts, images, mood changes, situations, or behaviors. Jose begins to scream and threaten his mother. Demanding items such as specific foods and not getting them. Angry face. Feeling sad and not recognizing this. Blaming mother for father's death. Throwing items out of frustration.			
List activities that the client can do to increase his or her coping ability or manage current thoughts and feelings. Listen to favorite music using headphones. Write in memory book about father. Color dinosaur coloring pages. Call grandmother Olga (insert phone number) for support. Go for a walk with neighbor Jason (who is an adult, insert phone number). Use belly breathing ("smell the pizza, blow in the pizza"). Work with Play-Doh.			
List people who can help the client cope with or manage his or her thoughts and feelings.			
Name: Grandma Olga		Phone #: 000-000-0000	
Name: Neighbor Jason		Phone #: 000-000-0000	
Name: Aunt Nina		Phone #: 000-000-0000	
List safe spaces where the client can go when a crisis is developing: Small tent in living room with blanket, must remain open. Grandma Olga's house, Grandma will pick up. Back porch, by the box of stuffed animals. Cuddle with dog in living room.			
These are the professionals or agencies to contact during a crisis.			
Clinician's name: Sandy Therapist **Phone #:** 000-000-0000			
Other OhioGuidestone Staff: Fred Supervisor **Phone #:** 000-000-0000			
Local Crisis Line Name: Local Crisis Line **Phone #:** 000-000-0000			
OhioGuidestone Crisis Line Phone #: Enter number for your region			
National Suicide Hotline Phone #: 1-800-273-8255			
Something or someone that is worth living for is: The dog, running with the dog, summer at the pool, Grandma Olga, having ice cream with her.			
Client Signature	Date	Staff Signature	Date
Parent/Guardian Signature	Date	Supervisor Signature	Date

Figure 18

As you can see, it is important to be as specific as possible. Use names, not just titles. This makes the plan more real. Be sure to insert phone numbers (and alternate phone numbers). List as many coping activities and safe spaces as you can. In a crisis situation, a place or person may not be available, and it is a good idea to have plenty of backup. Be specific about where and how dangerous items will be stored. Then, immediately help with securing the items. In this case, you would ensure that Jose's mother really does put all kitchen knives in the lockbox while you are there. You can then document in your case notes that all knives were secured.

Remind your client that a safety plan is a living document and that you will review and revise this plan with her as needed. Be enthusiastic about the safety plan. Don't think of the safety plan as merely a document; think of it as *the tool that helps your client stay safe*!

Once you have completed the safety plan with your client (and the parent if the client is a minor), the client (and parent) must sign it. Give your client/the parent a copy and make sure that it is posted in a prominent location. Submit your copy of the safety plan to your supervisor on the same day so it can be reviewed and filed electronically right away.

If a client refuses to sign the safety plan, you must inquire why. Here are some reasons why a client may refuse to sign a safety plan:

- The safety plan was not created collaboratively with the client. Revise the safety plan until your client feels it is truly hers and will sign it.
- Your client is not willing or able to commit to safety. Reassess client safety and consider the need to arrange for hospitalization.
- There is a power struggle between the therapist and the client. Remove this by stepping back, giving the client a new safety plan form, and letting her be in charge of it. Ensure that the safety plan contains realistic measures to prevent harm to self.
- If the client is a child and is too upset to sign, have the parent sign, as the parent will be the guide to safety at this point. Return the following day, review the safety plan, and have client sign.

Once the plan is signed, ensure again that your client is in a calmer state and is able to manage thoughts of harm to self or others. Ask:

- ***How do feel now about staying safe?***
- ***How are you going to use this plan?***
- ***What will you do if __________ happens?***

Help your client walk through potential challenges and triggers for suicidal thoughts that could occur in the next few days. Make sure that your client can explore calmly what he will do to stay safe. Be sure to once again help your client connect with his reasons to stay alive, keeping in mind that this should not be done in a way that increases feelings of shame, as shame can be an overwhelming feeling contributing to thoughts of suicide. Here are some do's and don'ts for identifying and reminding your client of his reasons to live.

Don't:

- Tell your client that he will ruin someone else's life if he commits suicide.
- Tell your client that his god will be angry with him if he commits suicide.
- Shame your client about not having enough friends or alienating family.
- Remind your client of relational failures.

Do:

- Remind your client of the love for (person or activity) that he talked about.
- Highlight how his face lit up when he talked about it.
- Wonder out loud what else he could do with (person) and how this would impact his life and the life of (person).
- Help your client explore how he can embody the values he implicitly explored with you.
- Remind your client that he deserves to live a meaningful, connected, and value-based life, just like all the people who are important to him.

If your client is a child, ensure that the parent is up to the challenge of overseeing the client's safety. The parent's state of mind and ability to manage his or her own emotional responses to the client's safety issues matters greatly. Ask:

- *Now that we have outlined all of these steps to keep your child safe, how confident are you that you will be able to do so?*
- *Is there still anything standing in the way of keeping your child safe? If there is, what is it? How can we overcome any barriers to keeping your child safe?*
- *Who supports you? In my experience parents often become overwhelmed when their child struggles with safety issues. This is natural. Because it is easy to become overwhelmed, it is important that we identify a reliable person to help you cope with the stress of this crisis. Who might this person be? Who could be a backup for that person?* (Post the names and phone numbers of the parent support persons in a prominent spot.)

If you determine that the parent is not presently able to ensure the client's safety, help the parent identify someone who can assist them. Contact that person, ascertain that he or she is willing and able to help, and incorporate the assistance this person will provide into the safety plan.

If you determine that the parent is unable to ensure the client's safety and the parent is unable to provide you with the name of a person who can help with keeping the client safe, you must call 911 and ensure that the client receive an emergency psychiatric assessment at the ER.

If you determine that the parent is neglectful or abusive toward the client, you must file a report with the child abuse hotline. You must provide the hotline with evidence of your allegation. Here is an example of a situation that requires a call to the child abuse hotline:

Seven-year-old Eduardo is threatening to jump out of the third-floor window of his home. His mother was able to talk to him and get him to move away from the window. When you arrive, Eduardo is crying and screaming. His mother's eyes are glazed over. When you speak with her she intermittently falls asleep, then wakes up again. Eduardo's mother is not able to provide you with any information about who could assist with keeping Eduardo safe. She is incoherent and repeatedly calls Eduardo "a little shit." Eduardo escalates again, this time threatening to run to the highway to get hit by a car. You need to:

- Call 911 right away.
- Place a call to the child abuse hotline. Be specific about your allegations and the child's inability to stay safe without support. Do this after the client is safely on the way to the ER.

These actions require you to immediately notify your supervisor and file an internal risk incident report. You will need to follow up regarding the client's disposition to ensure that he receives appropriate follow-up care once released from the emergency room or hospital. Keeping Eduardo safe will require collaboration with other providers and, in all likelihood, the local department of child and family services.

6. Follow-Up: Post-Crisis Intervention

> Services that are provided after the crisis, when the client is no longer in danger of serious harm to self or others, are essential to recovery. However, *post-crisis services are not billed as crisis intervention services.* Post-crisis intervention can include, but is not limited to: psychotherapy, therapeutic behavioral services (TBS), medication management, intensive outpatient services (IOP), and case management services.

When your client has received crisis intervention services, it is imperative that follow-up occur in a timely manner. Post-crisis intervention services help move the client beyond the crisis and serve as the basis of future crisis prevention. This is especially important if your client is frequently in crisis.

If your client's resources and skills are not sufficient to manage her challenges, post-crisis intervention must include:

- Resource building
- Skill building
- Ongoing safety planning/crisis prevention
- Collaboration
- Relationship building

- Values identification
- Meaning making
- Planning for living in spite of symptoms

Begin by quickly identifying resources appropriate to the situation or trigger that frequently precedes a crisis. Here is an example:

Brian becomes agitated easily, and when he becomes agitated he tends to think about suicide, especially if he is alone, which is most of the time. To help Brian you should:

- Identify a list of people Brian can call for support. This list should include people who are willing and able to visit Brian or ask him to come over to visit immediately. This list can include a mental health provider, but also Brian's natural supports (as opposed to only using professional supports).
- Identify a list of places Brian can go for support. One of these places could be a drop-in center for those who struggle with mental illness.
- Build a resource box for use in the home. It can contain books, music, a stress ball, images, letters, really anything that helps him build resiliency through connection.
- Begin skill building. Evaluate what has and what has not worked in the past. Find out what specific skills your client is lacking. Brian is not able to manage his suicidal thoughts. They become a threat to him and tend to take over this thinking. Hence, Brian has to learn to manage his suicidal thoughts. Because suicidal thoughts can lead to suicidal behavior (and perhaps Brian has had a prior suicide attempt), he needs to be taught specific ways to manage suicidal thoughts. He needs to be coached to use these skills, first in a role-play situation until he demonstrates mastery, then in real-life situations in the presence of a mental health worker, and lastly, once he is secure in using his new skills, when he is alone. It is easy to forget a step in skill building. Skills need to be learned and practiced in the company of a mental health provider until they become second nature. Only then is your client ready to use them in a real-life situation.
- Review the safety plan and incorporate new resources and skills.
- Confirm that Brian truly feels that the services address his needs and situation.
- Continue to build the therapeutic relationship to ensure that you know everything you need to know to ensure appropriate care. Say: ***If you are experiencing suicidal thoughts and you find yourself making a plan, I need you to tell me. I care about you and want to help you, and I can only do that if I know what is going on in your life.***

Help your client find meaning and purpose by identifying values and taking action based on those values. Remember the tipping point?

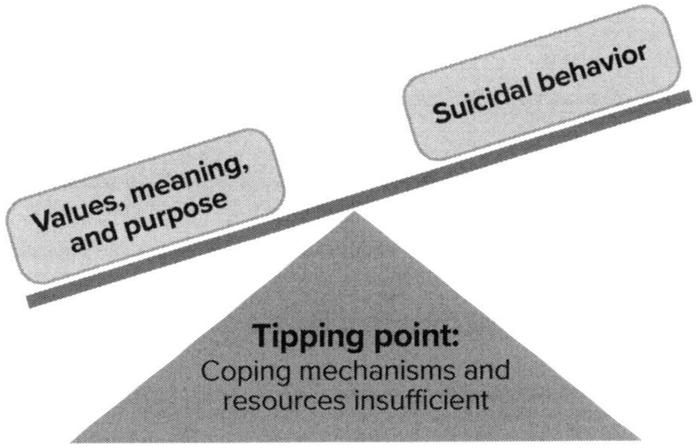

Figure 19

Your client's values, his sense of meaning and purpose in spite of significant mental health challenges, can tip the scale toward staying alive.

If your client continues to struggle with significant mental health problems in spite of appropriate evidence-based treatment, continue to help him work on symptom reduction, but also introduce the idea of living with meaning and purpose in spite of symptoms. Help your client build hope in the midst of symptoms and recognize that a meaningful life can overshadow them.

After a crisis, increase service frequency to ensure your client is not slipping back into crisis mode. Frequently assess for risk of serious harm to self, using the Columbia Scale, and, if needed, for risk of harm to others using a risk assessment for violence form. If at any point your client endorses thoughts, plans, and intent of serious harm to self and others again, then crisis intervention services must once again be provided until the imminent threat of harm to self or others has subsided.

Handle with Care: Building Workable Professional Lives

Our mission is to improve lives. In order to do so we, as mental health providers and human beings, must be well. When we neglect our own lives and needs, we run the risk of not being able to serve our clients in the best way possible. Because mental health providers in the community mental health setting often work with the most challenging clients, under difficult conditions, we must build resilience in our own lives. The following list of ways to build resilience (American Psychological Association, 2018) is designed for the general public but can easily be adapted for mental health providers:

Make connections. Good relationships with close family members, friends, or others are important. Accepting help and support from those who care about you and will listen to you strengthens resilience. Some people find that being active in civic groups, faith-based organizations, or other local groups provides social support and can help with reclaiming hope. Assisting others in their time of need also can benefit the helper.

Avoid seeing crises as insurmountable problems. You can't change the fact that highly stressful events happen, but you can change how you interpret and respond to these events. Try looking beyond the present to how future circumstances may be a little better. Note any subtle ways in which you might already feel somewhat better as you deal with difficult situations.

Accept that change is a part of living. Certain goals may no longer be attainable as a result of adverse situations. Accepting circumstances that cannot be changed can help you focus on circumstances that you can alter.

Move toward your goals. Develop some realistic goals. Do something regularly—even if it seems like a small accomplishment—that enables you to move toward your goals. Instead of focusing on tasks that seem unachievable, ask yourself, "What's one thing I know I can accomplish today that helps me move in the direction I want to go?"

Take decisive actions. Act on adverse situations as much as you can. Take decisive actions, rather than detaching completely from problems and stresses and wishing they would just go away.

Look for opportunities for self-discovery. People often learn something about themselves and may find that they have grown in some respect as a result of their struggle with loss. Many people who have experienced tragedies and hardship have reported better relationships, a greater sense of strength even while feeling vulnerable, increased sense of self-worth, a more developed spirituality, and heightened appreciation for life.

Nurture a positive view of yourself. Developing confidence in your ability to solve problems and trusting your instincts helps build resilience.

Keep things in perspective. Even when facing very painful events, try to consider the stressful situation in a broader context and keep a long-term perspective. Avoid blowing the event out of proportion.

Maintain a hopeful outlook. An optimistic outlook enables you to expect that good things will happen in your life. Try visualizing what you want, rather than worrying about what you fear.

Take care of yourself. Pay attention to your own needs and feelings. Engage in activities that you enjoy and find relaxing. Exercise regularly. Taking care of yourself helps to keep your mind and body primed to deal with situations that require resilience.

Additional ways of strengthening resilience may be helpful. For example, some people write about their deepest thoughts and feelings related to trauma or other stressful events in their life. Meditation and spiritual practices help some people build connections and restore hope.

The key is to identify things that are likely to work well for you as part of your own personal strategy for fostering resilience.

The key to building and maintaining professional resiliency is to *have a life* outside of work and to maintain a healthy work/life balance. This balance is unique to each provider, and you should develop a sense of how it works for you over time and with the help of your supervisor. Additionally, incorporating principles of acceptance and commitment therapy (ACT) into the way we view our professional practice can be helpful.

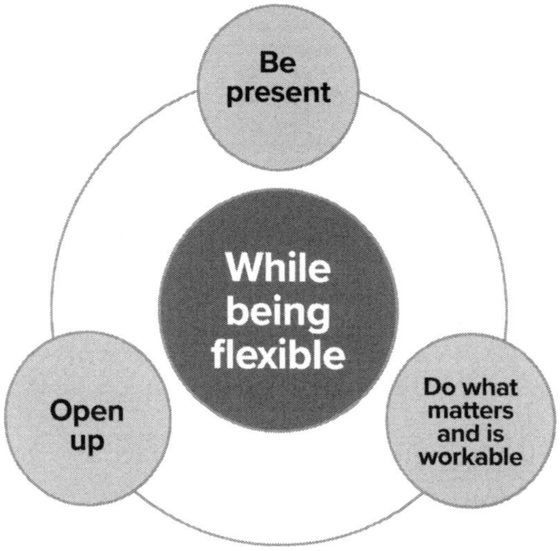

Figure 20. Adapted from Harris (2009).

Crises require us to be truly present, open up to the situation without becoming absorbed into it, and to do what matters most for the client. (which often is to get the client through the imminent crisis so he can keep living and building a meaningful life).

When we return from the crisis situation, our task is to also be present ourselves, to open up to the present moment and acknowledge that the crisis is over, and to do what matters for us so we can continue to live, work, and further build a meaningful life. Built into ACT (Harris, 2009) is the acknowledgment that we must do what matters in a way that is workable. Harris (2009, p. 225) calls workability "our best friend." Here are some things that are professionally not workable:

- Not having a personal life
- Working all the time
- Neglecting friends and family
- Being completely sedentary
- Thinking of oneself as capable of saving all

The following terms have been used in an attempt to describe what can happen when providers practice in a way that is not workable:

- Burnout
- Secondary traumatic stress
- Vicarious traumatization
- Compassion fatigue

What these terms have in common is that they all result from practicing in a non-workable way. As mental health providers we must achieve a sustainable work/life balance. Working all the time and neglecting our own health, families, and friends is neither sustainable nor aligned with the values that drive us to help others. Those values, of course, must also be applied in our own lives and to the way we construct our professional lives. Supervisors and coworkers play an important role in helping us create a workable professional life.

Even if you maintain a healthy work/life balance, crisis situations can impact the way you think, feel, and act over time. For this reason, you should schedule weekly supervision meetings with your supervisor. These supervision meetings should address more than just problems with workflow, productivity and paperwork issues. Each supervision session should contain a designated time to reflect on the impact of the work on the worker, and the impact of the worker on the work.

It is important to understand that the work we do when we provide crisis intervention will impact the way we feel. Ignoring or denying these feelings can contribute to maladaptive ways of coping.

Reflecting on the services we provide in stressful situations can help build resilience in the crisis intervention provider. Sherryl Scott Heller and Linda Gilkerson (2009) outline the principles of reflective supervision in their book *A Practical Guide to Reflective Supervision.* Reflective supervision relies heavily on creating safety in the supervisory relationship in order to enable the supervisee to explore all kinds of feelings about the work. The ability to reflect and to defuse from the work while also being immersed in it can improve the practitioner's ability to provide thoughtful, attentive, collaborative, and compassionate services.

Appendix 1: Situation Examples

John

John, a 15-year-old who identifies as male and Caucasian, reports in person that he is feeling so overwhelmed and hopeless that he stole rope from Walmart, picked out a tree in his backyard, and intends to hang himself tonight when his parents go to bed.

Is this a crisis per current State of Ohio definition?

Yes. The following assisted in determining that John is experiencing a crisis:

- John has thoughts of suicide.
- There are safety issues in his environment.
- His mental status includes feeling hopeless and overwhelmed.

Why is this a crisis (per current State of Ohio definition)?

John is experiencing a life-threatening situation and extreme emotional distress that calls for immediate action.

Should crisis intervention services (face-to-face) be provided?

Yes.

Per the Ohio Administrative Code, the primary goal of crisis intervention for John may be to reestablish safety. Activities to assist with reestablishing safety for John may include:

- Immediate stabilization.
- Deescalation.

The purpose of crisis intervention services for John may include:

- Connecting John to the most beneficial and appropriate services possible.
- Facilitating access and continuity of care, including safety planning.

Doug

Doug is a 17-year-old who identifies as transgender and Hispanic. Doug reports having experienced so much anxiety in the restroom stall around an hour ago that he picked at skin on a forearm until bleeding occurred.

Is this a crisis (per current State of Ohio definition)?

Probably not. The following could assist in determining if Doug is experiencing a crisis:

- Does Doug have thoughts of suicide? Doug answers, "No, I just wanted to snap out of it."
- Are there safety issues in Doug's environment? Doug answers that there are knives at home, but there's no intention of doing anything with them to create any further wounds.
- Is Doug experiencing overwhelming anxiety that prevents him from controlling aggressive impulses toward self or others due to this? Doug answers that the anxiety has lessened, that it comes and goes, and that it is usually related to gender. Doug shares that continuing to pick at skin until it bleeds may be helpful.

Why is this not a crisis (per current State of Ohio definition)?

Doug is not experiencing a life-threatening situation, and although he was experiencing elevated anxiety, he is not experiencing extreme emotional distress that calls for immediate action.

Should crisis intervention services (face-to-face) be provided?

No. Although crisis intervention services are not provided, Doug could still likely benefit from being connected to the most beneficial and appropriate services possible.

Doug, revisited

Doug is a 17-year-old who identifies as transgender and Hispanic. He reports experiencing increasing anxiety over the last 2 weeks. He stares blankly and states, "I feel worse than I have ever felt." Doug starts picking at multiple old wounds on both forearms until several start bleeding. Doug states, "I don't care if all my blood drains out."

Is this a crisis (per current State of Ohio definition)?

Probably. The following could assist in determining if Doug is experiencing a crisis:

- Does Doug have thoughts of suicide? Doug answers, "Maybe I should just die." He does not share anything further but does not deny intent to attempt suicide when asked.
- Are there safety issues in Doug's environment? Doug answers that there are knives at home and that he has recently started using them to cut when feeling anxious. Doug states, "I cut and pick all the time."
- Is Doug under the influence of drugs or alcohol? Doug does not answer, but there are no obvious signs of recent drug or alcohol use.
- Is Doug experiencing overwhelming anxiety that prevents him from controlling aggressive impulses? Yes, anxiety appears to be consistent with the level of Doug choosing to cut and pick at skin until bleeding occurs. Doug does not deny the intent to attempt suicide or that the purpose of cutting is to die.

Why is this likely a crisis (per current State of Ohio definition)?

Doug could be experiencing a life-threatening situation and appears to be experiencing extreme emotional distress that calls for immediate action.

Should crisis intervention services (face-to-face) be provided?

Yes.

Per the Ohio Administrative Code, the primary goal of crisis intervention for Doug may be to ease the crisis or to reestablish safety. Although Doug's lack of safety may seem vague due to the absence of a plan or intent, a need for immediate action is warranted. Activities to assist with easing the crisis and reestablishing safety for Doug may include:

- Assessment
- Deescalation
- Immediate stabilization
- Care planning

The purpose of crisis intervention services for Doug may include:

- Returning Doug to the usual level of pre-crisis functioning
- Connecting Doug to the most beneficial and appropriate services possible
- Facilitating access and continuity of care, including safety planning

Doug, revisited: documentation

Be sure to document clearly that Doug does not deny suicidal thought, plans, and intent. His lack of denial is what moves Doug's situation from being a problematic situation into being a crisis as defined by the Ohio Administrative Code. Additionally:

- Outline Doug's escalating symptoms: He has recently begun to use knives to harm himself and reports that he has never felt this bad before.
- He endorses not caring about dying after cutting himself. This means that his cutting should be classified as a suicide attempt requiring immediate intervention. However, it is *not* nonsuicidal self-injury (NSSI), because Doug has some intent to die.

Jennifer

The mother of Jennifer, a 9-year-old who identifies as female and African American, states over the phone that Jennifer is "having a crisis." Jennifer's mother reports that Jennifer is yelling, screaming, throwing things, jumping up and down, and slamming doors. Jennifer's mother states, "She always does this when I'm about to watch *Real Housewives*! She needs to be sent somewhere!"

Is this a crisis (per current State of Ohio definition)?

Probably not. The following could assist in determining if Jennifer is experiencing a crisis:

- Does Jennifer have thoughts of suicide? Jennifer refuses to get on the phone; her mother states, "No, she's never tried anything like that."
- Are there safety issues in Jennifer's environment? This could depend on what Jennifer is throwing. Is she throwing items that could be considered dangerous such as knives, hammers, screwdrivers, glasses, or boiling water? Jennifer's mother reports Jennifer is throwing toys, mostly stuffed animals. Also, what is Jennifer yelling? Is she making threats of harm to self or others? Her mother reports that Jennifer is screaming, "I hate you!" Jennifer is not reportedly making any threats.
- Is Jennifer experiencing overwhelming anxiety that could prevent her from controlling aggressive impulses toward self or others due to this? No. Although Jennifer is upset, apparently that her mother is watching a particular TV show, anxiety leading to difficulty controlling aggressive impulses does not appear to be present.

Why is this not a crisis (per current State of Ohio definition)?

Jennifer is not experiencing a life-threatening situation or extreme emotional distress that calls for immediate action.

Should crisis intervention services (face-to-face) be provided?

No. Although crisis intervention services are not provided, Jennifer could still likely benefit from the following:

- Connect Jennifer, her mother, or both to the most beneficial and appropriate services possible.

Paul

Paul is a 12-year-old who identifies as male and biracial. Mr. Smith, Paul's homeroom teacher, shares that he has concerns because Paul has written the words "Suicidal Tendencies" and "Negan Must Die" all over a notebook. Mr. Smith also shares that he has overheard Paul telling classmates that he just finished reading *13 Reasons Why* and that he can relate to the book.

Is this a crisis (per current State of Ohio definition)?

No. "Suicidal Tendencies" is the name of a thrash band, Negan is a character in the *Walking Dead* comic book and TV series, and relating to *13 Reasons Why* may mean many different things to Paul. It would still be beneficial, though, to follow up just to make sure Paul is not experiencing a crisis by determining the following (Mr. Smith could assist by providing his perspective):

- Does Paul have thoughts of suicide? He reports none when asked.
- Does Paul have thoughts of wanting to harm others? He reports none when asked.
- Are there safety issues in Paul's environment? He reports none when asked, and none are evident.
- Is Paul experiencing overwhelming anxiety that could prevent him from controlling aggressive impulses toward self or others due to this? No.

Why is this not a crisis (per current State of Ohio definition)?

Paul is not experiencing a life-threatening situation or extreme emotional distress that calls for immediate action.

Should crisis intervention services (face-to-face) be provided?

No.

Appendix 2: Selected Figures

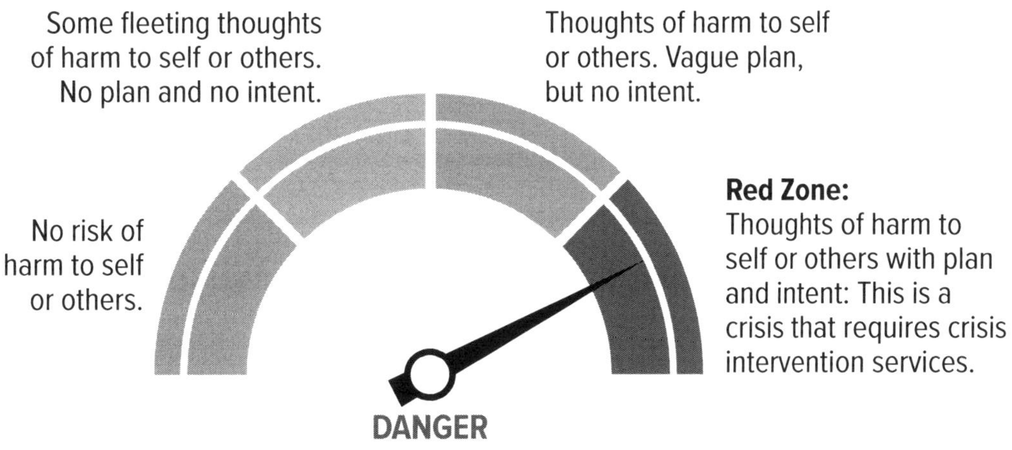

Figure 5

Six-Stage Crisis Intervention Model
1. Rapid assessment, including lethality assessment. *Billable crisis intervention services (face-to-face) begin.*
2. Identifying major problems or crisis precipitant: the tipping point.
3. Identifying feelings and emotions: active listening, validation, co-regulation, reframing.
4. Generating and exploring alternatives: connect and collaborate about plans.
5. Implementing an action plan: establish safety through agreed-upon means (can be removal of access to lethal means, hospitalization, supervision of client by parent, etc.). Beginning meaning making. *Billable crisis intervention services have concluded.*
6. Follow-up: post-crisis intervention

Figure 9

Depression pulls
me back this way.
Being active moves
me this way.
Where I am right now
Where I want to be

Figure 17

References

American Psychological Association. (2018). 10 ways to build resilience. The road to resilience. Retrieved from http://www.apa.org/helpcenter/road-resilience.aspx

Centers for Disease control and Prevention. (2016). Adverse childhood experiences. Retrieved from https://www.cdc.gov/violenceprevention/acestudy/index.html

Centers for Disease Control and Prevention. (2018a). Suicide rising across the US. Retrieved from www.cdc.gov/vitalsigns/suicide/index.html

Centers for Disease Control and Prevention. (2018b). YRBSS results. Retrieved from www.cdc.gov/healthyyouth/data/yrbs/results.htm

Columbia Lighthouse Project/Center for Suicide Risk Assessment. (2016). The Columbia suicide severity rating scale: Supporting evidence. Retrieved from http://cssrs.columbia.edu/wp-content/uploads/CSSRS_Supporting-Evidence_Book_2018-02.pdf

Columbia Lighthouse Project. (2016). C-SSRS for communities and health-care. Retrieved from http://cssrs.columbia.edu/the-columbia-scale-c-ssrs/cssrs-for-communities-and-healthcare/#filter=.general-use.english

Duty to Protect, 5122-3-12 (2018). Retrieved from http://codes.ohio.gov/oac/5122-3-12

Harris, R. (2009). *ACT made simple*. Oakland, CA: New Harbinger.

Heller, S. S., & Gilkerson, L. (Eds.). (2009). *A practical guide to reflective supervision*. Washington, DC: Zero to Three.

Jackson-Cherry, L. R. & Erford, B. T. (2018). *Crisis assessment, intervention, and prevention* (3rd ed.). New York, NY: Pearson.

James, R. K., & Gilliland, B. E. (2017). *Crisis intervention strategies*. Boston, MA: Cengage Learning.

Klonsky, E. D., Victor, S. E., & Saffer, B. Y. (2014). Nonsuicidal self-injury: What we know, and what we need to know. *Canadian Journal of Psychiatry, 59*(11), 565–568.

Lewis, J. S. (2015). Crisis intervention with HIV-positive women. In K. Yeager & A. Roberts (Eds.), *Crisis intervention handbook: Assessment, treatment, and research* (4th ed., pp. 578–598). New York: Oxford University Press.

Peterson, J., Freedenthal, S., Sheldon, C., & Andersen, R. (2008). *Nonsuicidal self injury in adolescents. Psychiatry* (Edgmont), *5*(11), 20–26.

Ohio Administrative Code. (2018). OAC 5160-27-12(A). Community mental health agency services. Retrieved from http://codes.ohio.gov/oac/5160-27

Roberts, A. R., & Ottens, A. J. (2005). The seven-stage crisis intervention model: A road map to goal attainment, problem solving, and crisis resolution. *Brief Treatment and Crisis Intervention, 5*(4), 329–339.

Schore, A. N. (2016). *Affect regulation and the origin of the self: The neurobiology of emotional development.* New York: Psychology Press.

Schore, J. R., & Schore, A. N. (2008). Modern attachment theory: The central role of affect regulation in development and treatment. *Clinical Social Work Journal, 36*(1), 9–20. doi:10.1007/s10615-007-0111-7

Substance Abuse and Mental Health Services Administration. (2009). *Practice guidelines: Core elements for responding to mental health crises.* HHS Pub. No. SMA-09-4427. Rockville, MD: Center for Mental Health Services, Substance Abuse and Mental Health Services Administration.

Substance Abuse and Mental Health Services Administration. (2018). Adverse childhood experiences. Retrieved from https://www.samhsa.gov/capt/practicing-effective-prevention/prevention-behavioral-health/adverse-childhood-experiences

Yeager, K., & Roberts, A. R. (2015). *Crisis intervention handbook: Assessment, treatment, and research.* New York: Oxford University Press.